FROM STONING TO ENTHRONING

Recipes to Walking in *Jesus-Style* Honor

GREGG DENNINGTON

ISBN: 978-1-66786-710-6
eBook ISBN 978-1-66786-711-3

Cover design: 100 Covers
Printed in the United States of America

ENDORSEMENTS

Gregg Dennington sent me the manuscript of his newest book, *From Stoning to Enthroning*, and I was so excited to dive in that I sat down immediately to look over a couple of chapters. Well, twenty-some chapters later, I realized I'd just read the most amazing book on honor I've ever read.

Gregg's writing style drew me in and I was enthralled. I almost cried several times (which I never do) and I laughed out loud many times (which I almost never do) from the wonderful stories and how they relate to a healthy culture of honor. I so enjoyed how Gregg took a valuable topic and presented it in such a simple, straightforward, helpful, and fun manner.

Thank you, Gregg, for ministering to me in these pages. You helped me see many areas in my own life where I haven't genuinely honored others. But you did it in a non-condemning way. And then, of course, you showed me how to do it the right way.

I haven't read a book in years that's been as enjoyable and helpful as *From Stoning to Enthroning*. I highly recommend it.

Roger Traver
President of Mountain Top Marriages

From Stoning to Enthroning is a powerful book filled with short stories, illustrations, and nuggets of gold that go right to the heart of what it means to "honor all people." Presented in an easy-to-read format, Gregg's latest book both inspires and challenges, answering all the right questions. What does Jesus-style honor look like? Why is it so important? What do we need to change about our own thinking and actions to walk this path of love? You nailed it, Gregg! Thank you!

Michael Heath
Director of YWAM Frontier Missions, Northeast Asia

From Stoning to Enthroning takes you on a journey to not only grasp the meaning of living an honor-filled life, but also equips you with how to walk that life out. I cannot think of a better suited individual to be the tour guide on such an important journey. And, as with all great tour guides, Gregg keeps you connected with his many stories that showcase the honoring lessons the Lord has etched out in his own life.

This book is perfect for the brand-new believer as well as the seasoned saint, and should be at the top of everyone's must read list! I see *From Stoning to Enthroning* as a pebble being dropped into calm waters, the tiny ripples soon becoming a massive tidal wave. It is just what the church needs, and is perfectly on time!

Amy Mahoney
Executive Director of KC Keyholders, Inc
Author of *Living Life with the King*

If you want to be inspired to overcome adversity and hardship when it seems impossible, then I highly recommend Gregg Dennington's book, *From Stoning to Enthroning: Recipes to Walking in Jesus-Style Honor*. It contains beautiful and fascinating stories from Gregg's life about honoring others, valuing our true identity, and the incredible power of forgiveness. His testimonies of how to take the higher road in responding to life's challenges will empower you to do the same. You, and those you influence, will be glad you read this book.

Steve Backlund
Co-Founder, Igniting Hope Ministries
Associate Director, Bethel Leaders Network

The atmosphere of heaven is honor. In His humanity, Jesus perfectly modeled this for us. *From Stoning to Enthroning* beautifully clarifies how to live an internal and external life of honor in today's often rancorous society. This is a book that gently demands a response. I offer my highest recommendation for this well written and perfectly timed work. Thank you, Gregg. Please keep writing!

Amelia Gaillard, MAPC

Once again, I was challenged and encouraged by one of Gregg's books—this time, his latest offering, *From Stoning to Enthroning*. Just like previous books, Gregg's blend of humor, vulnerability and straight-shooting truth made the reading enjoyable while also convicting. Several times as I read, I found myself thinking of relationships in my own life where I needed to apply the principles and values he lays out.

Gregg has a gift for illustrating and explaining truth while also keeping it immensely practical; he doesn't let you get away with simply nodding your head in agreement, you've got to search your heart for application! I'm convinced that if more of us would apply the principles he puts forth in this book, our churches and communities would be changed for the better.

Scott Contival
National Director, Youth With A Mission Taiwan

If a definition of honor is "to show a courteous regard for," then the way Gregg's new book *From Stoning to Enthroning* is presented radically embodies that truth. A forgone conclusion? Not necessarily. Other authors might write, "you should, you must, you're evil if you don't ..." and poke you in the eye with a stick. Gregg uses the honor truths he knows so well to provide *and* empower you so that you *want* to be more like Jesus.

He also often reminds you of your own value which propels you to esteem others more. With brilliant stories, pertinent examples, and his own life experiences—along with a delicious sense of humor—*From Stoning to Enthroning* takes you on a journey of knowing what honor is, how it's displayed in practical ways, and how vitally necessary it is in today's world.

This author can write about honor because he has sown (and reaped) it professionally and personally for decades. We have known Gregg for many years, and an unmistakable characteristic that marks his life is a continual lifting up of others. He sees the flecks of gold in them and refuses to focus on the dirt.

Reading and imbibing this book will give you exactly what the title describes. It is not an exaggeration. We have been transformed to love and exalt others better through these pithy chapters and the living example of the author. Thank you, Gregg, for writing this book!

Paul and Susan Kummer
Pastor, Bethel School of Supernatural Ministry,
Redding, CA
Authors of *Equipping the Saints: Raising Up Everyday*
Revivalists Who Sustain the Move of God
(Destiny Image Publishers)

Come on now, is honor really that big a deal? Honor? Really? Well, after reading Gregg's latest book, *From Stoning to Enthroning*, I am persuaded that this kingdom value is absolutely critical to our Christian faith. But fair warning: This book is easy to read yet deceptively powerful. While journeying through its pages, there were times I laughed out loud, times I shouted "amen!", and times I even cried. I was both convicted and challenged. I pray that you take this book, read it often, and learn to walk in the time honored biblical truth of honor. Turns out it is that big a deal.

David Jones
Lead Pastor, Cross Points Church, Kansas City

In his new book, *From Stoning to Enthroning*, Gregg opened my eyes wide open to the importance of honor. And he does so gently, guiding us to a place where we desire to honor all people, to see them just as Jesus sees them. He then goes on to share his own failures and successes to illustrate the joy and beauty of valuing all those created in God's image, especially those that society has conditioned us to cast aside. Or maybe even harder, the ones who've hurt us or the ones who just seem evil. This is a book I will keep close as a frequent reminder and challenge to always choose honor.

Sandy Gould
Team Leader, End Bible Poverty Now
(YWAM Colorado Springs)
Former Director, Oral Bible Storytelling (Seed Company)

Wow! From the first words of the introduction to the last words of the last chapter, Gregg knocked it out of the park. *From Stoning to Enthroning* will convict and usher in a reformation of your heart. A reformation that will lead you into activating the Jesus in you to get out of you and into your culture!

Our words create worlds, and Gregg has released hope that we can all be conformed into the image of our Father's Son. This is a book for those who are tired of a mediocre spiritual life and serves as a challenge, as well as an invitation, into Christlikeness. Thank you Gregg for baring your soul as you heard the voice of the Lord.

From Stoning to Enthroning is worth your time to read and read again!

Randy Hill
Senior Leader of Summit Church
Regional Facilitator for International Bethel
Sozo Organization
Author of *Encounters: Stories of Healing* and
Where Do I Fit?

DEDICATION

To the members of the Hakka Church Planting Team, the most remarkable missionary team I've ever seen: Your honor and humility and grace made you who you were back then and is forever stamped on the hearts you poured yourselves into. Including my own. What a powerful legacy!

FROM
STONING
TO
ENTHRONING

Recipes to Walking in *Jesus-Style* Honor

GREGG DENNINGTON

CONTENTS

INTRODUCTION

C an you imagine being in the Temple courtyard when the scribes and Pharisees dragged the adulterous woman before Jesus? Sensing the woman's fear and shame? Hearing "The law says we should stone her!" gauntlet thrown at the Creator's feet? Can you imagine feeling the tension as Jesus stooped down and wrote on the ground, refusing to acknowledge the woman's accusers? Seeing the looks on their faces as He stood back up and tossed His own "He who is without sin …" gauntlet before them? Can you imagine experiencing the stone-cold silence as the men, one by one, began to slip away? And then, witnessing the grace and compassion from Jesus' lips that set this adulterous captive free? Can you imagine?

I like to think I would have been one of the detached onlookers that day, but my past experience betrays me. It's entirely possible I would have been numbered among the finger-pointing mob of scribes and Pharisees. I've chucked more than a few stones in my life. Harsh, critical, demeaning, hurtful words (or actions) aimed right at the hearts of those around me. Stones designed to destroy. Stones that no follower of Jesus should ever throw.

Good thing our Father left a solution. One that delivers us from the bondage of a stone-throwing heart. One that enables us to launch others into their kingdom destinies. One that sets us on a journey *From Stoning to Enthroning*.

Here's how it's expressed in I Peter 2:17. "Honor all people." Don't let its size or simplicity fool you, this is one of the most profound commands in the Bible. Might also be one of the most challenging. Might also be one of the most powerful. In your hands, Jesus-style honor has the potential to propel those around you into the freedom, healing, joy, and security that God has for them. And as a faithful steward of this calling, you will experience the blowback blessings of healthier relationships, greater impact, abundant favor, and deeper intimacy with the very Author of kingdom honor.

From Stoning to Enthroning is composed of short, easy-to-read chapters designed to help you walk out this amazing journey. Small bites of a big meal. You'll learn what honor is, what it looks like in everyday life, tools to help you become an expert, obstacles that can spoil your success, and secrets to honoring the hard to honor. That said, the main purpose of this book is not information, but transformation. Where your values change, your thoughts change, your desires change, your beliefs change, and your words and actions change. Information is nice, but *From Stoning to Enthroning* is shooting for radical, life-changing transformation.

And now, for a timely warning. When some of you discover what this book is all about, you might begin to feel a few pangs of jealousy or self-pity. (Sorry, it's true.) Instead of thinking how *From Stoning to Enthroning* could help you become a more honoring person, you might be tempted to turn to the dark side, considering how it might help others do a better job of honoring you. "I want that! Don't I deserve to be more honored and respected and valued in life? I think I'll buy this book for my husband, my children, my friends, my boss, my coworkers, my neighbors, and all my small group members at church!" As the author of this book, a writer who hopes to sell a million copies, I'm going to say something I might regret. Please don't buy this book for other people. Don't send them as Christmas gifts if your goal is to help others honor you better. I encourage you instead, read this book for yourself first. With the goal in mind of becoming the most honoring person in your circle of relationships. (And then, by all means, please, please, please go buy this book for everyone you know.)

Now, I don't want to leave you hanging if you're one of those who struggles with wanting others to honor you more. Jesus gives us the secret to receiving honor in Luke 6:38. "Give, and it will be given to you. For by your standard of measure it will be measured to you in return." The best way to get honor is to give honor. One more time now, a bit more slowly: The best way to get honor is to give honor. And the book you're holding in your hands right now will help put you on this journey.

I hope you enjoy *From Stoning to Enthroning*. More than that, I hope you experience and embrace all the power in its pages. Now, go grow some honor!

CHAPTER ONE

PRICE TAGGED

❦

You've gotta love garage sales. The goal isn't really to make money, it's to get rid of all the junk in your house. Stuff you don't use anymore. Stuff that's broken or outdated. Stuff you're too uneasy to give to charity or toss in the trash. So, you organize a little day market in your driveway and try to sell it all. Cheap.

In 2007, a woman in New York state bought a plain, beige bowl for $3.00 at a neighborhood garage sale. A few years later, sensing something special about the purchase, she had it appraised. Turns out the bowl was a rare, thousand-year-old piece of Chinese pottery from the Soong Dynasty. A treasure that later sold at auction for just over 2.2 million dollars.

Something keeps bugging me about this story, something I can't get out of my brain. Boy oh boy, did someone put the wrong price tag on that bowl. News media interviewed the auctioneer, the wealthy buyer, and, indirectly, the woman who found the bowl at her neighbor's garage sale. They were all, of course, ecstatic. But can you imagine for a moment how the original owner must have felt? You know, the one who grabbed it off her mantle, took it out to one of the tables set up on her driveway, and stuck a price tag on it. For $3.00. Proud that she was finally going to get rid of the plain, beige bowl that never saw a Corn Flake in its life.

Can you imagine how this woman must have felt when she saw how much the bowl—her bowl—was really worth? Do you think she still has nightmares about slapping a $3.00 price tag on that plain, beige bowl?

There's something else that keeps bugging me, something else I can't kick out of my brain. Boy oh boy, how often we do the very same thing with one another. How often we're guilty of sticking the wrong price tags on the human treasures in our lives. $3.00 tags on priceless works of art.

Please don't cringe at the idea of putting price tags on people. God actually calls us to do it. The main Greek word for "honor" in the New Testament (*timao*) conveys the idea of value or price. It refers to how much something is worth. When God commands us to "honor all people" in I Peter 2:17, He's calling us to put His price tag on them. To esteem them the way He does. To determine their value according to His standards instead of the world's. And here, of course, is the rub.

Our natural bent is to assess a person's value based on the world's yard stick. Education, beauty, social position, wealth, intelligence, talents, titles, and accomplishments. (Feel free to add your own.) Our society screams that these are the things we should value in life; these are the standards we should use to judge others. But understand, when God calls us to "honor all people," He expects us to value them the same way He does. He expects us to put His price tag on them instead of our own.

It would be so much easier if we weren't under the spell of the world's thinking, wouldn't it? You know what I mean. Just walk into a room of a couple hundred perfect strangers and notice what happens when your price-tagging radar hums to life. Who would you rather hang out with: A polite, well-groomed, smart-as-a-whip, success story, or a foul mouthed, dumb-as-a-post, drug addict? Who would you most naturally esteem: A sympathetic, empowering, mother-of-the-year candidate, or a rude, condescending, know-it-all? Who would you stick the higher price tag on: A thoughtful, compassionate, defender-of-the-weak, or a callous, morally bankrupt, bully? Be honest now. Any of these people offend your tender sensibilities?

Every day, you are sticking price tags on the people you encounter. In your home, at work, on the streets, in your neighborhood, on social media. What kind of price are you tagging them with, God's or the world's? To answer this question, and to learn what a lifestyle of kingdom honor demands, you'll need to discover the truth about how your Father views the "all people" of "honor all people." Stay tuned.

CHAPTER TWO

FEARFULLY, WONDERFULLY

H enri Nouwen was a world-renowned theologian and lecturer who served for twenty years as a professor at Notre Dame, Yale, and Harvard universities.[1] He published 39 books which sold more than 7 million copies worldwide in thirty different languages.

Adam Arnett was a severely disabled young man, completely dependent on the care of others. He couldn't walk. He couldn't talk. He couldn't dress, eat, bathe, or use the restroom by himself.

In 1986, Professor Nouwen felt that God was calling him to work at the special care home where Adam Arnett lived. Almost every day for the next 14 months, he spent his mornings serving this young man. He woke Adam up, took off his

---

1 Henri J.M. Nouwen, Adam: God's Beloved (ORBIS, Anniversary Edition, September 25, 2013)

pajamas, shuffled him to the bathroom, shaved him, gave him a bath, dressed him, combed his hair, took him to the kitchen, helped him eat breakfast, brushed his teeth, put on his coat, cap, and gloves, sat him in his wheelchair, and rolled him over to the care home's day program. And during all these morning routines, Adam never spoke or reacted to Nouwen. Not once. He didn't smile when Nouwen did something well or frump when he didn't. No acknowledgment. No encouragement. No appreciation. No response whatsoever.

One day, a good friend of Professor Nouwen dropped in for a visit at the care home. When this man, also a pastor and teacher, witnessed Nouwen's morning routine with Adam, he got angry. "Henri, is this how you're spending your time? Did you resign your job at the university for this? For Adam? Why don't you leave this work to those who are better qualified? Surely you have more important things to do with your life!" Nouwen was stunned as he realized that his old friend, a man he loved and respected, had stuck the wrong price tag on Adam.

Most of us feel compassion for the Adams of this world, but do we count them valuable enough to give our lives for? Nouwen considered it a great privilege, a high calling, a holy passion to spend his life serving Adam. Because he knew— better than his good friend—what made Adam so valuable in God's eyes.

According to Genesis 1:27, God created us "in His own image." Wish I could tell you exactly what this means, but it's far too mind-blowing for me. Somehow, in some deeply mysterious way, every person on the planet is made in the image of the all-knowing, all-loving, all-powerful Creator God of the universe. His likeness stamped on their souls.

Here's what Nouwen had to say about Adam's value. "Adam bore silent witness to this mystery, which has nothing to do with whether or not he could speak, walk, or express himself, whether or not he made money, had a job, was fashionable, famous, married or single. It had to do with his being. He was and is a beloved child of God." When Professor Nouwen looked at Adam, he saw God's cherished son, created in His image for His amazing purposes. He saw God's likeness stamped on this severely disabled young man, a treasure precious enough to spend his life for. What a fantastic example of honor. The same kind God has called every one of us to.

Let's ratchet this up a notch, haul it into real life. Honoring the Adams of this world is one thing, honoring those hard-to-honor people in our lives is another. The challenge that comes with God's call to "honor all people" is that we don't like all people. Could be their political views. Could be their religious views. Could be their moral views. Could be their rotten attitudes or selfish thinking. Or it could be the big one, that they just don't like us. Something made obvious by their hateful words and actions. They've hurt us, rejected us, demeaned us, bullied us, abused us, shamed us, or shunned us. Face it, some people are harder to honor than others. Far harder.

If we want to "honor all people" the way God has called us to, we need to believe the staggering truth that they are fearfully and wonderfully made. In His image. Drug dealer? Made in God's image. Adulterer? Made in God's image.

Drunk driver, wife beater, corrupt politician? Made in God's image. The ones who continue to hate you, insult you, drag your name through the mud? Made in God's image. That image may be stained, shattered, or marred beyond recognition, but it still cries out. And God still cries out. They are His beloved creation, designed for His purposes, carrying His divine likeness on their souls. Which makes them worthy targets of honor. Your honor.

CHAPTER THREE
WORTH EVERY PENNY
⌒⌒⌒

W hen I was a kid, I'd often run down to the local drugstore for an after-school treat. Sometimes it was a Cherry 7Up, sometimes a ten-cent pack of baseball cards and the sad chewing gum that came with them. Who knows when I lost interest in baseball cards? Who knows what I did with all my old cards? And who knows why some of those old cards are now so valuable?

Take the 1909 T206 Honus Wagner baseball card. Only about 50 copies exist today. In 2016, one of those copies sold for a record 3.12 million dollars. And I can't help but think, "Has the world gone bonkers?!" Now, I know Honus Wagner is considered one of the greatest baseball players of all time. And I know this particular card is in good (for its age) condition. And I know it's extremely rare. But let's boil this down a bit. It's a tiny piece of old, cheap cardboard with a funny looking picture of Honus on the front and some statistics on the back. And (pause as some of you take offense) it's based on baseball. Baseball! A ball and some bases. Now I know that sports are important to some of us, but really? 3.12 million dollars for a baseball card?

All whining aside, I'm forced to agree that this old, cheap baseball-related piece of cardboard is worth every penny of the 3.12 million dollars that was paid for it. Why? Because that's how much someone was willing to pay for it. This is true for Van Goghs, vintage cars, rare coins, first edition classics, and ancient Chinese bowls. It's also true for people. All people. Easy-to-honor people and hard-to-honor people. They're worth whatever someone is willing to pay for them. Want to know how valuable the "all people" of "honor all people" are? Care to speculate what price tags are stuck on their lives? No guesswork needed. We already know their value because we already know the price that was paid for them.

In Matthew 13:44, Jesus described Himself as a man who discovered treasure hidden in a field. When He realized how precious the treasure was, He sold everything He owned in order to buy the field so He could claim the treasure. Simple story. We know the field is a picture of the world and the treasure a picture of us, but let's stop and consider the cost for a bit. Jesus sold everything He owned in order to purchase the world. He laid down His attributes as God, left heaven for a fallen creation, put on the frailty of human flesh, and surrendered His life on the cross. All to save mankind from sin and death. Price paid. World bought. Treasure claimed. Which means that God views "all people" as valuable as the cost His Son paid when He came and died on the cross for them. Priceless. "You know that you were not bought with things that can pass away, like silver or gold. Instead, you were bought by the priceless blood of Christ." (I Peter 1:18-19, NIrV)

And if you're wondering whether or not this is only for believers, check out I John 2:2. "He gave his life to pay for our sins. But he not only paid for our sins, He also paid for the sins of the whole world." (NIrV) Jesus paid the price for the "all people" of "honor all people." Since He died for them, they're stamped with this same astounding value as well. Priceless.

This is huge because we sometimes find these treasured people on our worthless people list. Our hard-to-honor list. These are the ones with repulsive political, moral, or religious opinions. These are the ones who don't like us, who've hurt, maligned, rejected, or demeaned us. And Jesus, who paid the price for them, considers them priceless.

This is huge because now we need to call into question the way we view these bought-with-a-price treasures of God. Now we need to recognize that the value He's stamped on their lives is often heaven and earth different from our own and makes them worthy of honor.

This is huge because we are now compelled to appreciate our high kingdom calling. To move to that place where we treasure every one of these hard-to-honor people the same way God does. Bought with an astounding price. Worth every penny.

This is huge.

CHAPTER FOUR

GUARANTEED

I n 2015, an art appraiser from Bonhams Auction House in London went to an apartment to look at a couple pieces of artwork the owners were curious about. While passing through the kitchen, she spotted a painting that was being used as a notice board. Small Christmas decorations were pinned to the bottom of the ornate frame, while letters, postcards, bills, and photos were tucked between the frame and the canvas, covering the lower third of the painting. The appraiser said she almost laughed when she saw the notice board because she recognized it as a well-known painting by South African artist, Irma Stern. A painting that would eventually sell at auction for over a million dollars.

We know very little about how the owners reacted to the news, but I guarantee you one thing. When they found out the painting's true value, they changed the way they treated it. I guarantee you they stopped using it as a notice board. I guarantee you they got rid of all the letters, postcards, bills, photos, and Christmas decorations. I guarantee you they moved it out of their kitchen to a much safer place. I guarantee you they didn't let their kids, grandkids, or family pets anywhere near it. I guarantee you they started treating this special painting like the treasure it truly was.

It's easy to be overwhelmed by God's call to honor all people, especially when we accept that this includes the hard-to-honor. It seems like an absurdly difficult task to step out in practical acts of honor for these individuals when deep down all we want to do is chuck stones at them.

We can always try to fake it; put on a polite smile, say the right words, do the right things for the wrong reasons. But that only put us in the Pharisee camp. Here's how Jesus described them in Matthew 15:8: "This people honors Me with their lips, but their heart is far away from Me." We may think it's better than nothing, but the consequences are profound. You and I simply cannot afford to be in a place where our honoring lips and actions live in a different zip code than our hearts.

Good news is, there's a far better way than Phariseeing it. In Luke 12:34, Jesus said, "For where your treasure is, there your heart will be also." When you see the treasure, your heart will follow, and so will your desire to honor. Let's grasp this powerful truth. The way you view someone is the way you'll treat them. If you don't think a person is very valuable, you'll end up treating them like a cheap notice board. But if you recognize their true, God-given value, you'll treat them like the million-dollar masterpiece they really are. And honoring words and actions will naturally flow from your heart. Genuine, heartfelt, honest.

Several years ago, a young Christian named Lisa[2] joined one of the ministry teams in our church. It didn't take too long for my wife, Eva, to notice that Lisa was a bit skittish in her commitment to serve on the team. Over the next couple of years, this charming, gifted woman went through duck-and-run cycles, fleeing her connections and responsibilities every time something went sideways in her life.

As you can imagine, this was frustrating for Eva, who often wondered if it was worth it to keep pursuing Lisa in the midst of all her messes and run-for-the-hills episodes. Wouldn't it just be better to cut her loose from the team? Wouldn't it be smarter to stop wasting time and energy on this broken, confused, irresponsible woman? Wouldn't it be easier to agree with some of the prevailing views already making the rounds? "Train wreck." "Will never change." "Beyond repair."

And then, my wife began to hear from God. Whenever one of these low-view opinions tried to sneak into her heart, the Holy Spirit would immediately shut it down and show her the hidden treasure He saw in Lisa. Things Eva couldn't yet see in real-life but still chose to believe. Until finally, God's view of Lisa became Eva's view of Lisa. Until finally, her eyes were opened to the truth that this ratty looking notice board was actually a priceless masterpiece. Which changed the way she started treating her.

---

2 Name has been changed

Eva began to believe in Lisa, refusing to give up on her when things got messy. She began to prophesy over her, giving her glimpses of what God saw in her life. She began to invest more time in her, not less, because she knew Lisa would grow to become powerful someday. She worked to protect her, not allowing any wonky thing to come in and destroy her destiny. Eva saw the treasure in Lisa's life and made sure others began to see it, too. She encouraged her, spoke purpose over her life, sowed hope in her heart, and empowered her to become the woman God wanted her to become.

This is what honor looks like. And it has had a life-shifting impact on Lisa. She learned to face her messes instead of fleeing them and has become powerful in the process. She now walks in greater passion, boldness, faithfulness, and a prophetic anointing that encourages all in her path. Her relationships have blossomed. People love to have her on their team. And her servant heart is off-the-charts incredible, making her a leader's dream. Lisa has transformed from Miss Mess to Can't Miss.

When you begin to value the people around you the way God values them, you will begin to treat them the way He wants you to treat them, to honor them the way He wants you to honor them. And they will begin to see what you see and believe what you believe. With powerful results. Guaranteed.

CHAPTER FIVE

EYES ON THE PRIZE

O ver the past few years, I've watched several episodes of a T.V. show about a bunch of men digging for gold in the Alaskan wilderness. The scenery is beautiful, the men rugged and colorful, but the show is far too boring to end up on the Emmy carpet. That's because one of its main characters is dirt. Loads and loads of dirt. To find just ten pounds of gold, mostly flakes and tiny nuggets, the men have to excavate about 25,000 tons of rock and dirt. 25,000 tons! That's a lot of time and effort for a medium-size jar full of gold. But few of the men complain about these results because ten pounds of flakes and tiny nuggets is worth around $250,000.

One interesting observation. The men have zero enthusiasm about all the dirt they're digging. Zero. They don't sit around and think about it, discuss it, cuss it, criticize it, or whine about it. They only have eyes for the gold. Just a few flakes in the sieve and these tough, hardworking men turn into giddy little boys. All smiles over this tiny bit of treasure. Pure excitement about what the next ton of dirt will reveal. They only have eyes for the gold.

Don't know about you, but sometimes I'm more interested in the dirt than the gold. That's where my eyes naturally turn, where my focus often falls. Put me in downtown Taipei traffic and I'll notice, and complain about, every driver's faults and failings. Too slow, too fast, too inconsiderate, too inattentive, too crazy, too close, too pushy, too timid, too lost. I hate to admit it, but I see dirt, not gold. And not just behind the wheel. My fault-finding, finger-pointing, dirt-spotting tendencies have reared their nasty heads at work, home, church, and online.

Maybe it makes me feel better about myself when I spot the faults and failures of others. Maybe I see it as some kind of payback for those "others" who've offended me. Maybe I was raised in an environment where dirt-finding was valued. Maybe it's a personality type gone off the rails. Maybe I just love the power of being a card-carrying member of the dirt patrol. Whatever the reason, this is a mindset I can't afford, a mindset that wars with my high calling to honor all people.

Here's a simple starter truth that's helped me experience greater victory in the battles: It's far more effective to focus on trying to see gold than on trying not to see dirt.

Back in my college days, I ran across *The Inner Game of Tennis* by Tim Gallwey. One of the main principles in this book was the idea that most of us learn a sport based on "don'ts." "Don't swing so early." "Don't point your left foot at that angle." "Don't start your backswing so high." Gallwey wrote that focusing on the "don'ts" makes us more susceptible to actually doing them. He once showed Johnny Carson, an avid tennis player, how this worked. On the set of the Tonight Show, Gallwey set up a cardboard cutout of a man. He then told Johnny, "Whatever you do, don't hit that man with the tennis ball. You can come close if you want, but do not hit that man." Racquet in hand, Carson dropped the ball, took his swing, and, of course, nailed the cardboard cutout. (Twice in a row, if memory serves.)

I once saw this at work on the racquetball court, with painful results. My friend, a gifted tennis player, was trying to get the hang of this four-walls-and-a-ceiling sport. I warned him several times how dangerous it was to turn around and run toward me when I had a shot, but his tennis habits wouldn't let go. I extended grace several times, pulling my shots when I saw him headed my direction. Didn't want to hit him in the face. Or worse. Finally, my patience gone, I decided to stop pulling my shots. The next time I saw him running right at me I let loose, the whole time thinking, "Don't hit him. Don't hit him. Don't hit him." Which, of course, I did. Nailing him right in his tender sensibilities. My conscious "don'ts" became my subconscious focus which became a (regretful) self-fulfilling prophecy.

Pop psychology aside, this lines up beautifully with the divinely inspired counsel Paul gave in Philippians 4:8. "Finally, brethren, whatever is true, whatever is honorable, whatever is right, whatever is pure, whatever is lovely, what-ever is of good repute, if there is any excellence and if any-thing worthy of praise, dwell on these things." Want to be righteous? Dwell on these positive things. Notice there's not one "don't" that he calls us to dwell on.

If you want to put an end to all your dirt-spotting tendencies, don't focus on ending your dirt-spotting tendencies. Focus instead, on learning to spot the gold. A character quality, talent, strength, attitude, gift, or passion. Look hard. Believe it's there. And when you find it, tiny though it may seem, stay focused on it. Because that's where the miracle will happen. That's where you'll hit paydirt, more gold than you could ever imagine. Can honor be far behind?

HAND-IN-HAND

∾

I f you read my first book, *From Groaning to Owning*, you might remember that I have a bit of a crush on Antiques Roadshow. That's the PBS show where people bring their household hopefuls into a large hall with professional appraisers trying to determine what's treasure and what's trash. Lots of interesting history. Lots of high expectations. Lots of chatty, know-it-all experts. What's not to love?

My first introduction to Antiques Roadshow took place on YouTube. A video about an elderly farmer who brought in an old American Indian blanket that had been lying around his house. The expert appraiser quickly got the farmer's attention by telling him that when he first laid eyes on the blanket, he almost stopped breathing. "I've never seen anything more important come through these doors." Turns out the farmer's old blanket was worth half a million dollars.

I want you to imagine for a moment that you've just walked through the doors of a huge hall where Antiques Roadshow is being filmed. And you're not coming empty-handed. Standing beside you is one of those hard-to-honor people in your life. Maybe it's someone who hurt you. Maybe it's someone you can't stand because of their loudmouth views on politics or theology. Maybe it's someone you don't like because you know they don't like you.

So, who are you dragging into this make-believe scenario right now? Your choice. No big rush. (Pause while you give this some serious thought.) Have you figured it out yet? Who did you choose to bring onto the floor of the Roadshow? What's their name? Can you picture their face? If yes, then you're ready to go.

You walk up to a table where an expert appraiser waits for you. It's Jesus, of course. He smiles and asks what you've brought in to have evaluated. You point to the hard-to-honor person beside you, not sure why you even bothered. Jesus looks him over and begins to ask you some questions. Basic stuff at first. Name, age, job, family, hobbies. Then He stops and asks the big question. "How much do you think he's worth?"

You know the right response, the biblically correct answer, but you still want to make your case. Jesus hasn't heard enough yet. He doesn't know the whole story about this guy and what he's done. So, you begin to point out all the flaws, faults, and failings you can think of. The selfish motives, crass behavior, disgusting morals. And you give example after example after example of how this person has hurt you and others.

All the time, Jesus just sits and nods, seeming to agree with everything you're saying. Of course He does. He knows exactly what awful things your hard-to-honor Roadshow companion has done. Finally, the Expert interrupts. "You never did answer My question. How much do you think he's worth?" You figure the answer is obvious but, with just enough venom, you say it anyway. "Not much, Jesus. Not much at all."

And that's when it happens. Jesus smiles. Not a sly, polite grin, but a full-face, all teeth on display kind of smile. "You don't understand," He says. "Sure, there are flaws—terrible flaws— but what you brought me today is a one-of-a-kind masterpiece! When I first laid eyes on him, I almost stopped breathing. He's priceless! And I should know, because I'm the One who paid the price! Can't you see it? Look closely, with a bit more faith this time. My Father's likeness is stamped deep in his soul. And again, I should know, because I'm the One who created him! You can't even begin to imagine the amazing plans, the powerful destiny I have for this treasure, can you? Please hear My heart. I've never seen anything more valuable come through these doors! Never!"

And there it is, laying open before you. Jesus' expert appraisal of this hard-to-honor person in your life. He sees all the flaws, faults, and failings, but He knows the truth you've had such a hard time seeing. This lost, marred, broken individual is God's treasured masterpiece. Graced with His signature. Bought at unbelievable cost.

I encourage you, if you struggle to obey Jesus' call to honor someone, stop for a moment, take that person by the hand, and lead them to the table of the only Appraiser that counts.

A few weeks ago, as I was writing this chapter, I decided to take my own walk through this special Antiques Roadshow. Problem was, I couldn't think of anyone to take with me. As best I could tell, none of my relationships fell on the unhealthy side of the honor scale. (It's amazing how many heart issues get cleaned up when you start writing a book like this.) So, I prayed, asking God to show me someone I struggled to value the way He wanted me to.

And there she was. Nancy Pelosi. (Yes, that Nancy Pelosi.) Democratic congresswoman. Speaker of the U.S. House of Representatives. Standing right beside me, clear as day, just inside the doors of the Antiques Roadshow. My gut said it all. I didn't like this woman. I didn't like her far-left agendas. I didn't like her smug attitude. I didn't like the things she said, or the way she said them. I didn't like the way she looked, cringing inwardly every time I saw her image pop up in a news clip. And I realized that my gentle, godly, pastoral heart was screaming, "What an evil, hateful woman!" That's right. About someone I've never even met.

I took Madame Speaker Pelosi by the hand and walked through the throngs of people right up to the table where Jesus sat. I already knew what He would say, but I still ran through the scenario in my mind. From my description of all her awful flaws, faults, and failings, to Jesus' unexpected smile and His glorious view of Pelosi. "One-of-a-kind masterpiece." "Priceless!" "My Father's likeness stamped deep in her soul." "Never seen anything more valuable come through these doors!"

The result was staggering. What began as a nice little thought exercise ended with a stunning revelation of Nancy Pelosi's true identity. I got a glimpse of just how much God esteems her. Which changed the way I now respond when I see her, hear her, read about her, or think about her. (Or, one day, meet her face-to-face.) Because "where your treasure is, there your heart will be also."

I encourage you, take this journey with someone you love to hate. It'll change your heart.

CHAPTER SIX

THE TRIUMPHAL ENTRY

ᨑᨕᨑ

The best definition of honor in the Bible is found in the Christmas story. Not the ones written by Matthew or Luke, but the one penned by Paul. In Philippians. Chapter two. The one before Jesus came down to earth and set up residence in Mary's womb. "Do nothing from selfishness or empty conceit, but with humility of mind regard one another as more important than yourselves; do not merely look out for your own personal interests, but also for the interests of others. Have this attitude in yourselves which was also in Christ Jesus, who, although He existed in the form of God, did not regard equality with God a thing to be grasped, but emptied Himself, taking the form of a bond-servant, and being made in the likeness of men." (Philippians 2:3-7)

Did you spot the definition? "With humility of mind regard one another as more important than yourselves."

More valuable. More esteemed. More priceless. Genuine honor is where we view others—all others—as being even more precious than we are.

Let's start by kicking the elephant out of the room. Notice that Paul didn't say other people are more valuable than we are, but that we are called to view them that way. Big difference. Points to an attitude we need to own, a mindset we're expected to adopt. "Regard one another as more important than yourselves." There it is. The best definition of honor found in the Bible.

There's something else you need to know. This Christmas story not only contains the best definition of honor in the Bible, it also contains the best example. An example we're expected to follow. "Have this attitude in yourselves which was also in Christ Jesus."

During the era of the Roman Republic, victory parades (called triumphs) were sometimes thrown in honor of generals who returned to Rome after leading successful military campaigns. The senate would first determine whether the commander was worthy of such an honor, and if so, the triumph was approved. This huge spectacle usually began at the Triumphal Gate with a procession of chained captives, including enemy kings, governors, and soldiers. Some destined for execution. The spoils of war soon followed, cart after cart after cart of gold, silver, and precious works of art. Rome's senators and their servants entered next, walking the whole four-kilometer parade route on foot. And then came our star of the show, the victorious general riding in an oversized chariot pulled by four horses. Throngs of cheering spectators lined the streets as the man of honor passed by, knowing that on this one day alone he was promoted to the status of a demigod. The most highly esteemed mortal in Rome. Other parade participants followed the general's chariot, including soldiers, family members, singers, dancers, and exotic, never-seen-before animals. The triumph lasted all day. Sometimes two. All in honor of this one man.

I should probably mention that it was the general himself who submitted his name to the senate as being worthy of such a grand honor. And it was the general himself who organized every aspect of the event: the parade route, decorations, order of procession, entertainment, which treasures to display, which captives to kill. And it was the general himself who usually paid for it all. That's right. Almost every general so honored by a Roman triumph threw the parade for himself.

Which brings us to the Christ of the Christmas story. King of kings. Lord of lords. Not just a demigod for a day, but the Creator God who laid aside His divine attributes to don the trappings of human flesh. Try to imagine the mindset of this staggering moment. The humble attitude that compelled Him to regard others as more important than Himself. No proud, self-serving, glory craving here. This is the story of a true triumphal entry. The greatest example of honor the world has ever seen.

Which begs one very important question. Who was Jesus honoring when He made this mind-boggling choice? Who did He regard as being more important than Himself, so much so that He stooped down to take on the form of a bondservant? The answer should be obvious. Uncomfortable, but obvious. On that very first Christmas, 2000 years ago, Jesus regarded you, and me, and all of mankind as being more valuable than Himself. When the Son of God became the Son of Man, He honored us all.

Mind officially boggled.

A GLIMPSE OF HONOR
BEING TAILED
∽∿∾

S ome years ago, our church attended a revival conference
in Taipei and discovered the Horizon Inn, a small, charming, inexpensive hotel with a great breakfast buffet. The
rooms were small, but the service was huge. The owner of
the hotel, a man named Ivan, would probably not call himself a Christian, but he centers his business on kingdom-style
honor. He has a special heart for serving underprivileged students around the island who have little opportunity for short
getaways to the big city. The same is true for blessing young
people who have physical or intellectual disabilities, making
sure they have a cheap (even free) safe place to stay for a rare
mini-vacation. Added to this, the baked goods served on the
breakfast buffet come from a bakery that only employs intel-
lectually disabled men and women. All to acknowledge the
true value Ivan sees in these young people. Which is one of
the reasons Eva and I have made the Horizon Inn our go-to
hotel in Taipei.

In mid-2017, Ivan discovered that I had advanced cancer when I stayed at his hotel while undergoing radiation treatments at a nearby hospital. He never forgot it. In October of that same year, I ended up in the same hospital having a surgical biopsy for a metastatic lesion on my skull. Somehow, Ivan found out about my situation, called our church office in Toufen, asked how I was doing and if I needed anything. Really? A hotel owner even thinks to do this?

Just a short time later, while visiting my Taipei doctor after the long hospital stay, I started having an awful reaction to a painkiller they'd given me. One of the sisters at our church called Horizon Inn, explained the situation, and asked if Eva and I could stay there that night. When we arrived at the hotel, I looked as terrible as I felt. The guys at the front desk, under orders from Ivan, only charged us $3.00 for the room that night. And boy oh boy what a night it was. I threw up violently the whole time, pretty sure everyone in the hotel heard all the horrifics. The very next morning, and the couple that followed, the Horizon Inn staff brought fresh fruit smoothies to our room, along with an assortment of other healthy snacks.

But the honor well hadn't dried up yet. A month or so after the hurling episode, I began a two-week regimen of radiation to clear up the lesion in my skull. Since treatments were every day, Eva and I, of course, stayed at our little home away from home. (Where Ivan still refused to charge us more than $3.00 a night!) One morning, while Eva was back in Toufen taking care of some church business, I rode the elevator down to the main street to try and find some kind of supplement the doctor wanted me to buy. As I strolled up and down the street looking for the medical supply store, I ran into a young woman who looked familiar but couldn't quite put her face to a place.

After a bit more wandering, I finally found the store, went inside, and started hunting for whatever it was the doctor wanted me to get. When I turned around to ask the clerk something, I bumped into the same woman I'd seen earlier on the street. This time, the face clicked. She was the Horizon Inn desk manager, a hotel angel who'd just been commissioned by Ivan to discreetly follow me around, make sure I was feeling okay, and able to find whatever I needed. And that's what she did. Talked to the store clerk, made sure I was buying the right thing, took it to the counter, and paid for it all. (Over my deaf-to-her objections.) Bag in hand, I then lined up behind her like a baby duckling and followed her back to the hotel elevator and up to my room. Where more fresh fruit smoothies and healthy snacks were waiting.

This is what kingdom honor looks like.

CHAPTER SEVEN
THE GREAT HINDRANCE

A few years ago, a woman in our church came up to my wife and asked her to pray for the arthritic pain in her hands. Eva prayed for the woman, but nothing happened. Pain level unchanged. She prayed a second time, and still no improvement. Just as she started to go for it a third time, Eva felt God nudge her to ask the woman a simple question. "Is there anyone in your life you haven't forgiven?" The answer came quick. She'd held a grudge against her mother for years. So, my wife went to work, guiding this precious sister to the freedom of forgiveness. After that, she prayed one more time and the pain in the woman's hands completely disappeared.

A beautiful miracle. And a valuable lesson about breakthrough. Unforgiveness is a huge hindrance to experiencing the power of God in our lives. A hindrance to breakthroughs in healing. And a hindrance, as well, to breakthroughs in honor. You can't honor someone you won't forgive.

Though "unforgiveness" is a word generally accepted in Christian circles, it's not recognized by most dictionaries. No worries. Here's the definition I'm going with for this word that's not really a word. Unforgiveness is a state of mind that refuses to pardon those who've hurt or offended us. A heart that's unwilling to give grace to the guilty. A heart that balks at wiping their sinful slate clean. It is, as you might expect, the very opposite of forgiveness. And Jesus is dead serious about forgiveness. Check out the bombs He dropped on His disciples regarding this issue.

"For if you forgive others for their transgressions, your heavenly Father will also forgive you. But if you do not forgive others, then your Father will not forgive your transgressions." (Matthew 6:14-15)

"Whenever you stand praying, forgive, if you have anything against anyone, so that your Father who is in heaven will also forgive you your transgressions." (Mark 11:25)

And who can forget how Jesus ended His parable about the unforgiving servant? "And his lord, moved with anger, handed him over to the torturers until he should repay all that was owed him. My heavenly Father will also do the same to you, if each of you does not forgive his brother from your heart." (Matthew 18:34-35)

Boom. Boom. Boom. Three of the toughest teachings ever uttered by Jesus to His beloved disciples. (Which includes you and me.) No gentle exhortations here; more like feet-to-the-fire warnings. All with one main point. "If you don't forgive others, God won't forgive you." Think this issue of forgiveness might be high on Jesus' kingdom values list?

New Year's Day, 1982, was a day that Jerry and Francine Watkins[3] will never forget. Their 18-year-old daughter, Sarah, was killed by a drunk driver. The young man behind the wheel, Mike Stevens, was convicted of manslaughter and DWI but was sentenced to just one year of community service. The Watkins, of course, were outraged. They filed a 1.5-million-dollar lawsuit against Stevens, an impossible burden for the guilty 17-year-old. So, Sarah's parents proposed a different kind of settlement. They offered to reduce the amount Stevens owed them to just 936 dollars. With a few stipulations. Every week, for 936 weeks, the young man was required to send them a one-dollar check. That's eighteen years. Same as Sarah's age when she died. And the one-dollar check was due every Friday, the same day of the week she died. The checks, every single one, made out to "Sarah Watkins."

The Watkins were obsessed with making sure Mike Stevens would never forget what he'd done to their daughter. They even took him to court four times when they didn't receive their weekly check. The fourth time, just before sentencing Stevens to thirty days in prison for his failure to pay, the judge asked what the problem was. After all, it was only one dollar a week. Stevens told him he was haunted by Sarah's death and tormented by the weekly check-writing reminders. Which is exactly what the Watkins were hoping for. Payback.

---

3 Names have been changed

Suffering for suffering. A crushing burden of guilt and shame aimed at destroying the one who destroyed them.

And three people ended up in horrible, soul-sucking bondage. The fruit of unforgiveness.

Then there's this ...

February 12, 1993, was a day that Mary Johnson will never forget. Her 20-year-old son was shot and killed by a young man named Marlon Green. Only 16-years-old, Marlon was convicted of second-degree murder and sentenced to 25 years in prison. As a Christian, Mary knew she was supposed to forgive Marlon, so she went through the motions of looking at the young man at his sentencing and declaring, "I forgive you." But she knew deep down that her heart wasn't in line with her words.

For the next twelve years, Mary struggled with unforgiveness. Every time she thought of Marlon, wave after wave of anger washed over her. "I was full of hatred. I saw him as an animal, and I wanted him caged. Locked up for the rest of his life." Mary knew it was wrong to feel this way. She knew this wasn't the kind of forgiveness Jesus called her to. One day, God whispered, "Mary, you need to repent for all the things you've said about this young man, and for all the horrible feelings you've had about him." He then continued, "Every time Marlon's name comes up, every time you hear it within yourself, I want you to say, 'I choose to forgive.'"

So began Mary's journey into true forgiveness. She soon requested a face-to-face meeting in the prison with her son's killer. Part of the reason was to test whether her forgiveness was genuine. At that first meeting, Mary told the young man,

"In the courtroom, I told you I forgave you, but I really didn't. Today, from the bottom of my heart, I want you to know that I truly forgive you." Then, they hugged. A long, heartfelt hug. And Mary felt something leave her. All the anger and hatred she'd felt for twelve years instantly disappeared.

Over the next five years, a special bond began to grow between Mary and Marlon. She became like a mother to him, and he became like a son to her. When he was finally released from prison, after serving sixteen years of his sentence, she threw him a big "Welcome Home" party. Marlon walked into a house full of people, who immediately ran over to hug him. People who knew this man had murdered Mary's son. Last time I heard, Mary and Marlon were next-door neighbors. She is a changed woman, delivered from all the hate and anger, living in the freedom of true forgiveness. And he is a changed man, delivered from guilt and shame, living in the freedom of a "family" who love and accept him.

Such forgiveness. Such freedom. Such honor.

CHAPTER EIGHT
FORGIVE AND FORGET

F orgiveness can sometimes be a tricky thing. I've noticed that when some Christians say they've forgiven someone, they don't really mean what Jesus meant. So, they can't possibly follow what Jesus said. Uttering a simple "I forgive them" is their guaranteed pass to meeting His standard of grace. Saying the right words is enough to ace the test. But just a reminder: God is the author of forgiveness. He knows everything about it. He knows exactly what it is, how it works, and what it does. Which is why we should pay close attention to His thoughts on it.

Ephesians 4:32 is a great place to start. "Be kind to one another, tender-hearted, forgiving each other, just as God in Christ has also forgiven you." Did you catch that? We need to forgive others the same way God has forgiven us. His kind of forgiveness should be our kind of forgiveness. We get a good picture of what that looks like in Hebrews 8:12. "For

40

I will be merciful to their iniquities, and I will remember their sins no more." One of the hallmarks of God's incredible mercy is that when He forgives, He also forgets. All part of the same package.

Just so you know, God is not forgetful. He remembers every little thing about every single one of us. Including our sins. So, since God doesn't have a memory problem, "I will remember their sins no more" must be referring to something else. The original Greek word for "remember" gives us a clue. It means to "bring to mind" or "think about." When God forgives you, He makes an astounding choice. "I will not think about your sins again. I will not bring them to mind."

I'm guessing most of you have heard someone say, "I forgive, but I'll never forget." Ever heard it from your own lips? Or your own heart? This phrase has become common wisdom, society's take on true forgiveness. But not God's. When He forgives our sins, He also forgets them. Forever. And no matter how difficult it may seem, we are expected to follow in His footsteps.

About twenty years ago, our mission's Leadership Team was in the final decision-making stage of a huge building project, so they asked us local ministry leaders to pray about the decision, hear from God, and come share our thoughts with them. When we arrived at the meeting, one of the main leaders reviewed the project vision, shared some updated details, and then asked for our feedback. He also reminded us that the project would only move forward with a unanimous thumbs up. That if any one of us felt a "no" or "not now" from God, the Leadership Team would shut the whole thing down.

So, one-by-one we went around the circle sharing a short report on what God had spoken to us and then a simple "yes" or "no" on whether we should continue with the building project. I was pretty much at the end of the circle, and this is what I heard. Yes, yes, yes, yes, yes, yes, yes, yes, yes, yes, yes, yes, yes, yes. (Can you feel the mounting tension?) That's right. My turn. I shared what I felt God had spoken and ended with a somewhat apologetic, "I don't feel God wants us to continue with the building project." In other words, "No."

It didn't take very long for the leader of the project to unload. And I can understand why. He'd put so much of his time and energy into accomplishing this vision, and now, my opinion was threatening his baby. So, he started scolding me, blasting my character, questioning my ability to hear God's voice, accusing me of having an agenda to stop the project. I was hurt, embarrassed, and confused. I only did what they'd asked me to do. The shock of his response was so overwhelming that I don't remember much else about the meeting. After a few consoling pats on the back from other attendees, I got on the bus to go home. And began to stew.

That night, I kept thinking over and over about what happened, growing more and more angry with the leader as I replayed the whole horror show in my mind. Sleep was one of the first casualties of my response. It's hard to drift off when your mind's at war. "How could he treat me like that?" "In front of everybody!" "I only did what they asked me to do." "Who does he think he is?" And I played out scenario after scenario in my mind of what I was going to say the next time I saw him. No wonder I didn't get much sleep.

After a few days of struggling with the hurt and anger, I knew I needed to forgive this leader. With the same kind of forgiveness that God forgave me with. So, I released him from the guilt of what he'd done to me. Tore up the list. Flushed it down the toilet. Wiped his sinful slate clean. But boy oh boy was it tough! Why? Because I kept remembering. Thoughts of what he'd said. Thoughts of how he'd treated me. Thoughts of how I was going to get justice. And as soon as I vowed not to think these thoughts anymore, they'd come sneaking back in. While brushing my teeth, taking a shower, eating breakfast, walking the dog, having my quiet time. But I kept on with the work of forgetting. I worked on refusing to allow these things to come into my mind. I worked on remembering them no more. And slowly it happened. Jesus-style forgiveness. Peace. Freedom.

This leader and I didn't see each other very much after that meeting, and I found out one day that he and his family had moved out of the country. Some years later, while I was teaching at one of our missionary training bases in the U.S., guess who I ran into? Out of the blue? In the hallway of the guest house? I gotta tell you, we had an amazing reunion. Not one ounce of hurt or anger or hate. Not one ounce of desire for payback. No apologies necessary or expected. It was like the whole incident never happened. We talked and talked and talked. Good talk. And I discovered during that week just how much I loved and respected this amazing man. Now one of my favorite people in the world.

The fruit of walking in God's kind of forgiveness. Forgive-and-forget kind of forgiveness.

I'll end with this fairly obvious nugget. The process of forgetting is not always easy. But you need to know and believe that every time you toss out an angry, painful, hate-filled thought—every time you refuse to obsess about the offender or the offense—your forgetting muscle is growing stronger. Which makes the next time easier. And the next. And the next. Resulting in genuine, powerful, fruit-bearing forgiveness.

CHAPTER NINE
JESUS-STYLE FORGIVENESS

That's right. Three chapters in a row on the topic of forgiveness. In a book about honor. That's because unforgiveness is pretty much the opposite of honor, an insurmountable barrier to valuing others the way God wants us to. We can't honor someone we won't forgive. And forgiveness, genuine forgiveness, sets us up for honor. Valuing those who are hard to honor. Those who've hurt us, shamed us, betrayed us, mocked us, or broken our hearts.

Which sounds a lot like what Jesus encountered on His way to Golgotha. Think about it. Jealous Jewish leaders plotted to kill Him. One of His twelve trusted disciples was a traitor, betraying Him for a few pieces of silver. The remaining eleven abandoned Him when He was arrested in the garden. Their presumptive leader, Peter, denied even knowing Him. Three times. Within earshot. Jesus was tried in a kangaroo court, unjustly convicted, and sentenced to death. He was mercilessly scourged by a bone-laced whip, chunks of flesh ripped from His body. And then, surrounded by a crowd, Roman soldiers stripped Him naked—completely naked—and nailed Him to a cross to die.

But that's not all. The cross itself was not nearly as towering as depicted in Hollywood movies. Jesus' feet would probably only have been two or three feet off the ground, putting His face within spitting distance of those who came to mock Him. So, they came. His hateful enemies. And they taunted Him, cursed Him, insulted Him, and yes, spat on Him. Full in the face.

At that moment, twelve legions of angels were standing at the ready in heaven, swords drawn, waiting for a word from their King. 72,000 warriors chomping at the bit to hear the word that would release them to come and dispense justice. "We're ready, King Jesus! Just say the word! Just say the word!" Finally, in the midst of all the abuse and cruelty, Jesus said the word. And all of heaven gasped. "Father, forgive them, for they don't know what they are doing." (Luke 23:34 NLT)

Think about it. Jesus forgave His enemies while they were still killing Him. He didn't wait for them to take Him down from the cross before He would forgive them. He didn't wait for them to cleanse His wounds before He would forgive them. He didn't wait for them to repent and apologize before He would forgive them. He didn't wait for them to promise not to hurt Him again before He would forgive them. Jesus forgave them all while they were still mocking, cursing, insulting, taunting, and torturing Him. While they were still spitting on Him. While they were still killing Him. This is God's kind of forgiveness.

Sadly, many of us set conditions on our forgiveness, and it sounds something like this:

"I forgive them, but I'll never forget what they did to me."

"I forgive them, but I will never trust them again."

"I forgive them, but they still need to pay for what they've done to me."

"I forgive them, but I'll never be close to them again."

"I forgive them, but first they need to apologize, show me how truly sorry they are."

"I forgive them, but I refuse to pray for blessing on their life."

"I forgive them, but I'm not going to help them succeed in life."

"I forgive them, but first they need to change the way they treat me."

"I forgive them, but I never want to see them again."

Here's an uncomfortable question: How would you feel if you discovered God was using your kind of forgiveness to forgive you with? "I forgive you, but ... I'll never forget what you did." "I forgive you, but ... I'll never trust you again." "I forgive you, but ... I'll never be close to you again." "I forgive you, but ... I'm not going to help you succeed in life." Wouldn't that be horrible? Praise God, that's not His way. That's not His standard of forgiveness.

Jesus' response on the cross is our great example to follow. "While we were yet sinners, Christ died for us." (Romans 5:8b) He forgave His enemies even while they were sinning against Him. Even while they were killing Him. His response? "Father, forgive them." And all of heaven gasped. So should we.

CHAPTER TEN

THE SILENT SLAM

ᓚᘏᗢ

There are many different guises that dishonor can take in our lives. Some are of the in-your-face variety. Hurtful words and harsh actions that are easy for just about anyone to spot. But some are far more subtle. Camouflaged by polite smiles and words, these expressions of dishonor often go completely unnoticed. Even by the ones using them. (That's us.) Sadly, I'm an expert at this. And I bet I'm not alone.

Years ago, I was attending our local mission's staff conference. The guest speaker that year was one of the top leaders of our international organization, a man I greatly respected. On the second day of the conference, I walked outside during one of our break times and spotted this leader nearby. Just standing there. By himself. All alone. Even though I was a pretty shy guy, I saw this as a great opportunity to go meet one of my heroes. Which is what I did. Walked right up and introduced myself. He looked up from something he was reading, a blank expression on his face, and asked, "So, what do you do here in Taiwan?" A bit nervous, but happy for the question, I told him I was helping to plant churches among the Hakka Chinese. He looked me in the eye and said, "You need to have one of my guys come and help you do it the right way." Then he looked down and started reading again.

Being savvy enough to know our conversation was over, I mumbled a quick "thank you" and walked away. Every bone in my shy, insecure, leader-pleasing body banged up and bruised. I wanted the respect of my hero. I wanted him to smile, pat me on the head, and say, "Gregg, you're doing a fantastic job here! Keep up the good work!" But that's not what I got.

And at some point during the next few minutes, I cut this man right out of my life. Without even thinking about it, and not really understanding what was going on, I came to the conclusion that he was a terrible leader I'd never respect or listen to again. It all happened so fast. The door in my heart slammed shut. And stayed shut.

Three years ago, I preached a five-week series on the culture of honor. Four days before my final sermon, I was walking up and down the streets thinking and praying and preparing. Asking God to give me an example from my own life where I had not been very honoring. He immediately brought this man to mind. A man I hadn't seen or thought about for at least fifteen years. And I got it. For the first time, I understood. Shutting this leader out of my life was dead wrong. A harsh, hurtful, dishonoring response. Just as grievous as any in-your-face approach. So, I repented. Right there on the street. Opening the door I'd slammed shut so many years earlier.

Like I mentioned, I hadn't seen or heard anything about this leader in a long, long time. Not even online. Well, two days after my repentance episode on the streets, I was scrolling through Facebook and spotted his picture on a 25-minute video teaching. What a test! This had the finger-prints of God all over it, and I couldn't help but laugh. As I sat and watched his teaching, I realized the radical change that had taken place in my heart when I finally opened the door. Honor was flowing again for this man. (For bonus points, care to guess what the topic of his teaching was? The consequences of cutting off people in our lives. Same topic I would teach in two days.)

A long story for a short point. We can't go around slamming doors on others every time they hurt us. I know, I know. It's a quiet, non-confrontational approach so subtle no one would probably even notice. An easy way to deal with the pain. You cut off the hurtful person, and you cut off the hurt. But it's not Jesus' way. He loves them, He values them, He sees the destiny He purchased for them on the cross. And He wants us to open the door of our hearts to these hard-to-honor treasures, just like He's opened the door to us.

"But I say to you who hear, love your enemies, do good to those who hate you, bless those who curse you, pray for those who mistreat you. If you love those who love you, what credit is that to you? For even sinners love those who love them. If you do good to those who do good to you,

what credit is that to you? For even sinners do the same."
(Luke 6:27-28; 32-33)

Love your enemies. Do good to those who hate you.
Bless those who curse you. Pray for those who mistreat you.
This is what open doors look like. This is what Jesus-style
honor looks like.

CHAPTER ELEVEN

DIFFERING VIEWS, DIFFERING VALUES
❦

Before moving on to the how-to's of honor, we should probably dip our toes into one more potential challenge. How can we possibly honor those who have very different moral, religious, or political values than we do? Different lifestyle choices? Different views on sexual issues? Different theological beliefs or church practices? Different stances on government policies?

And the big question: Won't honoring these people damage our Christian testimony? Won't our words and actions be seen as agreeing with their lifestyles and opinions? Won't our acceptance of them be seen as acceptance of who they are and what they believe?

Whether you know it or not, some of these questions might already be rattling around in your brain somewhere. Just waiting to become a barrier to honoring the hard-to-honor.

As a Christian, Dan Cathy, CEO of Chick-Fil-A, has some strong personal beliefs about whether it's acceptable for homosexuals to get married. And he's expressed these views publicly more than a few times. Enter Shane Windmeyer, founder and executive director of Campus Pride, a leading LGBTQ student organization in the United States. In 2012, homosexual activists criticized Cathy's statements on gay marriage and Chick-Fil-A's financial support of "anti-LGBTQ organizations and hate groups." Shane Windmeyer promptly led a national boycott of the fast-food chain.

Then Dan Cathy did something unusual. He reached out to Windmeyer in friendship, trying to better understand who he was and what his Chick-Fil-A struggles were all about. Of course, Windmeyer was cautious at first, knowing that their views were set in stone, poles apart. But Cathy persisted. Friendship was the goal. Understanding and honoring this homosexual activist, even in the context of extreme disagreement.

Windmeyer remembers the moment this all became clear. "I assumed that if I mentioned my husband to Dan that he would run from the room screaming, right? Or throw water on me. I'm not sure quite what I expected. But every [time] Dan had [the opportunity] to react negatively based on his beliefs, he extended a hand, a hug, a warm welcome instead. He role-modeled what his company has said they are, which is to treat people with dignity, honor, and respect."

Windmeyer went on to say, "A true, authentic friendship or relationship is built around fun, and engaging each other in things that you enjoy. Dan invited me to the Chick-Fil-A Bowl game, and he [also] invited my husband, who does enjoy football. I decided it was important. This was an opportunity to demonstrate what our friendship had become, which was a chance to laugh and enjoy college football."

Such a beautiful example of honor. From both men. And, as you might imagine, there was a harsh reaction to this blossoming friendship. Many LGBTQ activists were furious with Windmeyer, and many Christians with Cathy. Why? Because they didn't understand the truth that honoring those you disagree with doesn't mean you approve of their beliefs or lifestyle. Guilt by association is not kingdom.

Rick Warren frames it this way. "Our culture has accepted two huge lies. The first is that if you disagree with someone's lifestyle, you must fear or hate them. The second is that to love someone is to agree with everything they believe or do. Both are nonsense. You don't have to compromise convictions to be compassionate."

If we don't understand this, we're gonna have a tough, tough time honoring the hard-to-honor people in our lives. Jesus understood it. And He understood how the religious right of His day would respond. In Luke 7:33-34, He said, "For John the Baptist has come eating no bread and drinking no wine, and you say, 'He has a demon!' The Son of Man has come eating and drinking, and you say, 'Behold, a gluttonous man and a drunkard, a friend of tax collectors and sinners!'"

In case you didn't know, Jesus was a friend of tax collectors and sinners. Remember when He was invited to a dinner party thrown by His newly appointed disciple, Matthew? A party that included a boatload of detestable lawbreakers? In Luke 5:30, the Pharisees, after seeing Jesus accept the dinner invitation, "began grumbling at Jesus' disciples, saying 'Why do you eat and drink with the tax collectors and sinners?'"

And remember when Jesus invited Himself to dinner at Zaccheus' house, a tax man who was short in stature but big on cheating? When the people saw what Jesus had done, "they all began to grumble, saying, 'He has gone to be the guest of a man who is a sinner.'" (Luke 19:7)

Did you notice all the grumbling going on? All because Jesus was associating Himself with sinners. Why would He honor them with His presence at the dinner table? Why would He lavish His grace and acceptance on them? Did this mean He approved of their selfish, immoral, lawless ways? Get this. Jesus was a friend of sinners, even though He disagreed with their sinful lifestyles. And He made this honoring choice, knowing it would move the finger-pointing Pharisees to accuse Him of also being a sinner. Which they did. Guilt by association.

Honor all people. This is our calling. If a homosexual couple comes to your bakery and asks you to bake a cake for their wedding, do it. With love. With honor. That doesn't mean you have to write something on the cake that wars with your values, but you can sure bake them the best tasting, most beautiful wedding cake ever. Serve them with the same heart Jesus served the bride and groom who ran out of wine at their wedding in Cana. His focus wasn't on all the people who would get drunk on the wine He made, it was on honoring the bride and groom. By providing the by-far best wine at the wedding feast. Knowing that others would almost certainly call Him a drunkard for it.

I encourage you, don't let the fear of how others might respond keep you from honoring those who have different views, values, and lifestyles. Honor them with your grace, with your words, with your friendship, with your best. Just like Jesus did.

CHAPTER TWELVE

CLEANING OUT THE CUP

ᥫᥬ

A few years ago, I was teaching a sermon series on the culture of honor. As usual, I was walking down the street thinking, praying, and preparing. Sometime during that walk, I noticed how much I was distracted by those around me. Every person who threw trash on the ground. Every motorbike that passed me on the pedestrian-only sidewalk. Every car that ran a red light. Or made an illegal turn. Or roared by with a modified muffler that could be heard in the next county. Every fellow-pedestrian who crossed against the light. Every dog walker that let their precious pup lay land mines in my path. Every land mine they didn't pick up. Every land mine I almost stepped in.

In the middle of my less-than-generous observations, God spoke clearly to me. "What if those people you're thinking about right now could hear your thoughts?" Interesting divine interruption. Opened me up to imagine those around me wearing some kind of "thought radar" on their heads, able to hear all the opinions I had about them. Every judgment. Every rant. Every name-calling. Every burst of anger. Every sigh of disgust. Every unkind word.

God continued the sidewalk intervention by asking, "Would these people feel loved by what they hear? Would they feel accepted? Would they feel safe? Would they feel honored?" I'm pretty sure we all know the answers to these questions. The pain stabbed deep as I realized just how dishonoring I was. And just how destructive that could be.

I pride myself on being able to control my words, actions, and emotional expressions. Through the years, I've learned how to respond to difficult people and situations with a smile or a kind word or a gentle disposition. Good stuff. So out on that street, a few years ago, preparing for my sermon on honor, God reminded me how Jesus described the Pharisees in Matthew 23:25-28.

"Woe to you. Scribes and Pharisees, hypocrites! For you clean the outside of the cup and of the dish, but inside they are full of robbery and self-indulgence. You blind Pharisee, first clean the inside of the cup and of the dish, so that the outside of it may become clean also. Woe to you, scribes and Pharisees, hypocrites! For you are like whitewashed tombs which on the outside appear beautiful, but inside they are full of dead men's bones and all uncleanness. So you, too, outwardly appear righteous to men, but inwardly you are full of hypocrisy and lawlessness."

That one landed hard. Mostly because it was true. What I took great pride in was really a filthy cup and a whitewashed tomb. Beautiful on the outside (in my words, actions, and emotional expressions) but unclean on the inside (in my mind, thoughts, and feelings.) For the final lesson of the day, God showed me that I have a choice to either bless or curse others with my thoughts. So out on that street, a few years ago, preparing for my sermon on honor, this Pharisee repented. I made the choice to deal out honoring, blessing thoughts instead of disrespectful, cursing ones.

Now, to be honest, cleaning out the crud on the inside of the cup is not always an easy task. But there's hope. And that hope lies in Romans 12:2. "And do not be conformed to this world, but be transformed by the renewing of your mind, so that you may prove what the will of God is, that which is good and acceptable and perfect." We need transformation to take place. A change in our thoughts that comes through the renewing of our minds. Please note that it's not a passive miracle where we sit around waiting for God to do all the work. It's a partnership miracle. We do what He calls us to do, and He comes in with transformation power. Gracing us with the mind of Christ. (I Corinthians 2:16)

Your part of the partnership will take some grunt work. Start by saturating your heart with God-thinking. Make Philippians 4:8 your motto. Fill your mind with whatever is true, honorable, right, pure, lovely, reputable, excellent, and worthy of praise. And gentle reminder alert, these things don't just fall from heaven. Filling your mind requires action. Your action. Spend loads of time worshipping God, feasting on His Word, devouring kingdom teaching, and dwelling in His presence. Loads.

At the same time, and with the same passion, be sure to stop filling your mind with the garbage thinking and values of the world. Make tough choices about what you watch, read, and listen to. Proverbs 4:23 says, "Watch over your heart with all diligence, for from it flow the springs of life." Set a fierce guard over your heart that will no longer allow worldly pollution to come in and contaminate God's miracle work of renewal and transformation.

In pursuing your call to honor all people, especially the hard-to-honor, remember this: Honoring words and actions flow naturally from honoring thoughts. And honoring thoughts come from a renewed mind. This is where the battle begins.

A GLIMPSE OF HONOR
STANDING OVATION

ross Points Church in Shawnee, Kansas, is one of the most honoring churches I've ever heard of. Eva and I know this because we've been on the receiving end of this generous, encouraging, missions-minded fellowship for roughly thirty years now. I remember the first time we attended their annual Missions Conference activities held in November. On kick-off Sunday, about thirty of us missionaries, young and old alike, gathered outside the main auditorium doors. Waiting. And waiting.

Just after the service started, the doors eventually opened, and we entered an auditorium with flags from about every country in the world waving down at us from the high ceiling. One at a time, we began walking slowly down the long aisles to the front of the church. Lots of uncomfortable space between us. To be honest, with all eyes turned our way, and the applause beginning to grow, I was feeling a bit self-conscious.

Finally reaching the front of the sanctuary, we arranged ourselves on bleachers facing the congregation, just standing there smiling. Unsure what to do next. And that's when it happened. The growing applause turned into a wild, cheering, standing ovation. What probably lasted only one or two minutes seemed like twenty, and I remember one thing: Honor filled that auditorium. We could all feel it.

Too many missionaries around the world feel lost and forgotten by their sending or supporting churches, but not us. The welcome mat at Cross Points Church is huge and embracing and honoring.

That was only the beginning of this special conference. We were treated to a one-night retreat at a quaint little guesthouse, complete with a visiting speaker invited especially to encourage us. Another night was Ladies Night—according to them, the best event of the whole week. They were pampered by the sisters at Cross Points with a night of fun, sharing, and lots and lots and lots of gifts. Even a generous donation with specific instructions to go buy some new clothes. Just about every activity at the conference, including a special banquet at the end, was held with the purpose of celebrating—of honoring—the missionaries.

But I should probably point out that this honor is not relegated to one week in November. The church has special intercession teams that meet monthly just to pray for those of us on the field. Every month. Rain or shine. They stay in contact with us, hearing both our Praise Reports and our Prayer

Requests, and sending back any encouragement they feel we need. Refusing to let us feel forgotten! These faithful warriors have been standing with us for years, having a powerful impact in our lives and on the work we're doing. Kingdom honor in action.

And, of course, that's not all. The generosity and care that flow from this church is off-the-charts incredible. When we come back for furlough, they treat us like royalty. Renting cars for us to get around, pitching in to upgrade our computer needs, and making sure we have as many dinner invitations as we can handle.

There was the time in 2014 when Eva and I were back in Kansas City for a more extended visit. Our 25th wedding anniversary was near, and my dear wife was a bit wistful, having tried unsuccessfully to set up a little gathering of friends from the church to celebrate. (In Denmark, the honored couple always host their own celebration.) Early one morning, a few days after our actual anniversary, Eva and I were ushered into a car and told about a great new breakfast place in town we had to go check out. So off we went ...

... and couldn't believe our eyes when we pulled up to the restaurant. The outside of this little cafe had been decorated especially for us. Danish style! Complete with a floral arch erected over the entry and a dressed-out trumpet player doing his trumpet-playing thing. Now you need to know, my wife doesn't have a shy bone in her body. Not one. So imagine my surprise when she struggled to get out of the car and make her way into the cafe. Eyes trying to take it all in. Not sure what to say or do. Stunned. I remember having to pretty much push her through the doors—where we were greeted by about fifty of our friends who'd gathered together to celebrate our special milestone. Full of joy, laughter, speeches, food, and plenty of uniquely Danish traditions. I'm not sure Eva has ever fully recovered from this extraordinary act of honor.

And, of course, the honor shown by this church has not just been confined to heartwarming expressions or special events. There was the time when my parents passed away within a year of each other, and our Senior Pastor and his wife flew down to Dallas to attend both funerals. Doing whatever they could to support us.

And there was the time I had my skull biopsy in Taiwan. Both our senior and missions pastors immediately hopped on a plane, flew 7,500 miles, and hoteled it for a few days, just to make sure we were doing okay. Which meant having the tough talks with Eva, and listening to my sometimes inane rambling in the hospital room. As you can imagine, we felt cared for. Honored.

Now, I realize that this Glimpse of Honor might seem a bit mundane or ordinary. Not a whole lot of flash or sizzle. But that's exactly why I'm sharing it. I want to make sure you understand what mundane, ordinary honor looks like and just how powerful it can be. And just how within reach it is for all of us and all of our churches.

CHAPTER THIRTEEN
STICKS AND STONES

O ver the next few chapters, we're going to look at some practical, effective ways to honor others with our words. But first, we need to understand the enormous, soul-impacting power they carry. For good or bad. For life or death. Check out this children's poem I ran across decades ago. (Author unknown.)

Every plant has little seeds

That make others of its kind.

Apple seeds make apple trees

And they'll do it every time.

Seeds make flowers, shrubs, and trees.

Seeds make ferns, and vines, and weeds.

What you plant is what you grow,

So be careful what you sow.

Sir Winston Churchill, former prime minister of the United Kingdom, was famous for his sharp wit and even sharper tongue. On one occasion, his political nemesis, Lady Astor, told him, "If I were your wife, I'd poison your tea." To which Churchill responded, "Madam, if I were your husband, I'd drink it." Another time, a woman named Bessie Braddock chided a tipsy-looking Churchill, "Sir Winston, you are drunk!" "And you, Bessie, are ugly," Churchill replied. "But tomorrow morning I shall be sober, and you will still be ugly."

More than a few of us get a kick out of these stories, told sadly at the expense of Lady Astor and Bessie Braddock. I'm betting these two women didn't think Mr. Churchill's words were all that witty. And I'm betting you all know why. Words can hurt.

Whoever made up the little ditty, "Sticks and stones may break my bones, but words will never hurt me," didn't understand life at all. Words can hurt. Harsh words, demeaning words, accusing words, shaming words, mean-spirited words, manipulative words, slanderous words, dismissive words, scolding words, impatient words, belittling words. "Sticks and stones may break my bones, but words will never hurt me." Excuse me? Maybe someday we'll be secure enough to identify with this, but most of us are not there yet. Words can hurt. Whether spoken, written, delivered directly, or behind someone's back, hurtful words devalue. Which, of course, is the absolute opposite of honor.

"What you plant is what you grow, so be careful what you sow."

I encourage you to go back and read through the different kinds of hurtful words listed earlier. This time a bit more slowly, a bit more thoughtfully. Ever use any of these in the heat of an argument or a fit of anger? Ever use them when you're tired, sick, depressed, or discouraged? Ever use them while defending your pet political or religious view? Ever use them in response to others using them on you? Ever use them on Facebook, Twitter, or Instagram?

Here's what God thinks about the words we speak. "Death and life are in the power of the tongue, and those who love it will eat its fruit." (Proverbs 18:21) Eye-opening verse. We can sow words in others that are powerful enough to produce life or death. Easy choice, huh? Apparently not. You'd think that we, as Christians, would be the last people on the planet to sow words that produce death, right? Yet again, apparently not. Just think for a second about the times you've had other believers plant words of death in your heart. And take another second to think about the times you've planted words of death in the hearts of those around you.

"These people are brainwashed idiots."

"They're cowards [who are] afraid to do the right thing."

"What a moron."

"Anyone with a brain would get that."

"Biden is the idiot in charge."

"Brain-dead retard!!!!" (Yes, there were four exclamation marks.)

These are just a few of the death-inducing comments I ran across on Facebook or other website discussion boards. All posted by believers. Some who I know well.

"What you plant is what you grow, so be careful what you sow."

When I was in my early twenties, I was too shy to be a great conversationalist, so I began to depend on sarcasm. Trying to be the witty one in the room. I certainly wasn't as sharp as Winston Churchill, and (hopefully) not as mean-spirited, but I got pretty good at short, clever, under the breath put-downs. And since it usually received a few laughs, I kept working to improve my craft. Until it became part of my identity.

One day, God spoke clearly to me that my sarcasm was not honoring and had to go. Easier said than done. So, I grabbed hold of Psalm 141:3 and made it my daily prayer. "Set a guard, O Lord, over my mouth; keep watch over the door of my lips." It's hard to describe what happened next. I remember being at church one Sunday, standing in the lobby with my friends who were all chatting away, when a sarcastic put-down started to come out of my lips. All of a sudden, after just a few words, the guard that God set over my mouth took a stand. And I stopped speaking. Mid-sentence. All the other guys looking, listening, waiting for a punch line that would never come. Can't tell you how awkward that moment was for me. And it didn't stop there. For the rest of the day, the awkward moments just kept coming. Every time I got ready to fire off a sarcastic comment, the guard would take his stand and I would close my mouth mid-sentence. My closest friends probably thought I was having a stroke.

I can't remember how many weeks or months this struggle lasted, but in the end, the guard won. My cutting quips slowly came to an end. And I was free to honor others with my words instead of putting them down.

Might be a good place for some of you to start. Ask God to set a guard over your mouth every day, to watch over the door of your lips. And follow your watchman's lead as He helps you learn to control your tongue. So that, in the end, no unwholesome word would ever come out of your mouth, "but only what is helpful for building others up according to their needs, that it may benefit those who listen." (Ephesians 4:29, NIV) Sowing words of life instead of death.

"What you plant is what you grow, so be careful what you sow." Powerful poem. Something even a child can understand.

CHAPTER FOURTEEN

SHOOT FOR THE HEART

⌒ↄ◯ᴄ⌒

H is name was Joseph. Not the dreamer Joseph of multicolored coat fame. Nor the carpenter Joseph of Mary, Joseph, and Jesus fame. Nor the wealthy Joseph of short-term burial plot fame. This Joseph, a native of Cypress, was a pillar of the early church in Jerusalem. When radically-saved Paul was spurned by family, Pharisee friends, and a frightened, skeptical church, this Joseph took the young believer under his wing. And helped raise up the world's most powerful theologian and missionary. When John-Mark abandoned his three-person missions team, and was later snubbed by team-leader Paul, this Joseph took the young failure under his wing. And helped raise up a faithful, well-respected servant of God, one who would someday help the Apostle Peter pen the second book of the New Testament. This Joseph was so well-respected for his gift of encouraging those in the church, that the apostles gave him a new name. Barnabas. "Son of Encouragement." A man who valued others so deeply that he made it his mission to help empower them to be who God called them to be. Even the failed ones like Paul and John-Mark. Which makes this Joseph one of the most powerful men in the New Testament.

Paul knew firsthand the impact of this incredible expression of honor, which is why he challenged the saints at Thessalonica to "encourage one another and build up one another, just as you also are doing." (I Thessalonians 5:11) The Greek word for "encourage" in this verse is *parakaleo*. Sound familiar? It should. Jesus promised His disciples in John 14 and 16 that a Helper (*parakletos*) would come alongside to give them strength when He was gone. Which is pretty much the best picture we have of what it means to "encourage one another." To come alongside others and give them strength.

Some years ago, Eva and I were back in the States attending a church service when we ran into a worship team member at the water fountain. We didn't know her very well but had seen her singing on stage several times. After the normal church lobby pleasantries, I told her that we really appreciated her helping to lead worship. Then I mentioned that we loved how genuine she was onstage, and that her obvious passion for God had a huge impact on us. This woman looked at us for a second and began to cry, sharing that no one had ever said these things to her before. I was stunned by the impact of our brief encouragement drive-by.

I was stunned, as well, by the knowledge that her encouragement deficit occurred in a church filled with wonderful, caring, grateful, supportive believers. How could this possibly happen? I'm sure many people in the church loved this woman and had expressed appreciation for her serving on the worship team. But apparently, these expressions didn't deliver a deep enough wallop to her heart. Which begs the question, how can we make sure those around us get good and truly walloped by our words? How can we make sure our encouragement leaves a lasting, powerful, life-giving impact?

Here's the deal with encouragement: Any kind is better than none, but some kinds are more powerful than others. Deep-level encouragement leads to deep-level fruit. A sowing that nurtures the heart. Surface-level encouragement leads to surface-level fruit. It can make people feel good, but doesn't get far enough down to shift what really matters.

Whenever I walked up to the foul line during my high school basketball games, the cheerleaders would always chant the same thing. "Gregg, Gregg, he's our man! If he can't do it, nobody can!" Pretty nice, right? But even though I loved hearing this little ditty, thrilled that all those cute girls on the sidelines actually remembered my name, the cheer never really touched my soul. It wasn't personal enough. It never imparted true value. It never watered the roots of my budding identity. And it never helped me make the free throws.

"Way to go!" "Great job!" "Love what you're doing!" "Huge congratulations on winning that award!" Cheerleading others is good, certainly better than nothing, but it's not all that effective in imparting life. Appreciating others is also good. Very good. And certainly essential in building healthy relationships. "Thanks for taking the children to school every morning." "I really appreciate your help on this project." "Thank you for making dinner tonight." "I'm so grateful for your counsel." But again, its power to encourage on a deeper level is somewhat limited.

The key to encouraging others is simple. Focus on those hidden inner strengths that produce the obvious outer ones. Speak out what you love about their heart, their attitudes, their values, their personality, or their character.

When you notice your boss doing something well on a project he's leading, go ahead and start with the simple. "Great job on the project, John!" Then offer up something a bit more specific. "I really appreciate the way you're leading our team. You have such a gift for keeping us on task and helping us to accomplish our goals." But don't stop there. Shoot for the heart. "I especially love how patient you are with us. Even in the midst of our mess-ups and the looming deadline, you've had such grace with us. Thank you."

When you notice one of the children's workers at your church doing something well, go ahead and start with the simple. "Thank you for all you do in serving our children." Then offer up something a bit more specific. "Whether you're teaching or playing games or doing special projects, I've noticed how much the kids love being around you." But don't stop there. Shoot for the heart. "You carry such a spirit of gentleness and kindness, a spirit that reminds me of Jesus. I'm sure these are some of the things that draw the children to you. Thank you for being such an amazing influence!"

Start simple. Get more specific. Then, shoot for the heart.

I want to challenge you, be like Joseph! Yeah, that Joseph. Son of Encouragement Joseph. The incredible New Testament saint who valued others so deeply that he made it his life mission to empower others to be who God called them to be. Be like Joseph! Through the words you speak, the notes you scribble, the texts you type, and the Facebook, Instagram, Twitter messages you send.

Shoot for the heart.

A GLIMPSE OF HONOR
BLOSSOMING GOLD
❦

While grading the first papers of the semester for one of his senior level Bible College classes, Dr. Bruce Wilkinson spotted something unusual.[4] A wrinkled one-page paper that had clearly been crumpled up and then straightened out, the bottom right corner adorned with a ketchup stain. Dr. Wilkinson, curious about which student had handed in such a disaster, noticed the name Becky scrawled at the top. A name he couldn't attach to a face. Without hesitation, he gave the young woman a big fat F.

The very next class, Dr. Wilkinson searched the classroom, trying to put a face to the name. And there she was. Sitting in the back of the room. Her hair a mess, her clothes as rumpled as her homework assignment, her self-care in

_____

4 Dr. Bruce Wilkinson, *The 7 Laws of the Learner* (Sisters, Oregon, Multnomah Press, 1992) 112-114

serious doubt. Though the professor tried to connect with Becky during the lecture, she rarely met his eyes.

When the next assignments were handed in, he quickly found Becky's. No wrinkles or ketchup stains this time, but the paper still deserved an F. Dr. Wilkinson, however, did something few instructors would think to do. He stopped and prayed. "Lord, maybe Becky is supposed to be our project this semester. Would You give me the creativity and unconditional love to blossom her?" The first thing Dr. Wilkinson did was restrain himself from slapping an F on the paper. Instead, he wrote, "Dear Becky, I believe that this paper does not truly reflect your true talents and abilities. I can't wait to see what you can really do."

Her next paper improved to a D-. This time, the professor wrote, "Dear Becky, thanks for cracking the door just a bit. I didn't think I was wrong about you. How about the privilege of seeing what you can really do when you apply yourself? I'm on your team." Again, no grade recorded on the paper.

The next paper Becky handed in was two pages long. Worthy of a C. "Dear Becky, what a tremendous improvement! This paper is light-years ahead of your last and demonstrates incredible potential. I can't wait to see what your next paper's going to look like." Again, no grade.

Her next paper was four pages long, and very close to earning an A. "Dear Becky, your improvement is nothing less than astonishing! Your insights and the quality of your work are truly inspiring to me. I believe you are ready to show me everything you can really do." Once again, no grade.

Becky's next paper was far and away her best yet, so Dr. Wilkinson wrote, "Dear Becky, I'm now standing on the top of my desk cheering! I always knew you had it in you. I believe you're going to become one of our school's greatest Bible students, and it is a pleasure to watch you grow in my class." Then he scribbled a huge "A+" at the top. And just so you know, this Bible college professor was right about Becky. By the end of the semester, she was leader of the class.

Many years later, having lost contact with Becky, Dr. Wilkinson received a letter.

Dear Dr. Wilkinson,

I just had to write you a letter after all these years. You don't recognize my name because I'm now married. I don't know how to thank you. You are the first person in my entire life to ever believe anything good about me. Your class totally changed my life. I'm now happily married and have two wonderful children. I honestly believe that had I not met you and been in your class, I probably wouldn't even be married today. I don't know how I can ever thank you enough for believing in me.

Love, Becky

What a fantastic example of honor, of valuing others so highly that we use our words to grow the gold in them. That we use our words to build them, stir them, empower them, and inspire them. Or, as Dr. Wilkinson prayed, to "blossom" them.

So, at the risk of sounding pushy, where's your Becky?

CHAPTER FIFTEEN

FROM GOD'S LIPS

O ne of the most powerful practices in our "Honor All People" toolbox is prophecy. That's where we hear a word from God and pass it on to its intended target. Don't get nervous. The prophecy I'm talking about is not the kind usually dispensed by the likes of Isaiah, Jeremiah, Ezekiel, or Joel. These were Old Covenant prophets aiming at Old Covenant purposes. God speaking through these heroes to prepare and protect His rebellious nation until its Messianic destiny could be fulfilled. That's why their declarations were often harsh, scary, in-your-face heartstoppers, with just enough compassion thrown in to give their hearers hope.

You'll be glad to know that New Covenant prophecy is radically different. Different purposes, different priorities. In I Corinthians 14:3, Paul writes that the "one who prophesies speaks to men for edification and exhortation and consolation." Words from God that impart value to others. What we call honor. Now, you might occasionally run across a prophet stuck in his Old Covenant ways, declaring harsh "thus saith the Lord" judgments on those too slow to reach the exits, but these are (or should be) the exceptions. Paul points us to a higher way. A different spirit. Prophecies that edify, encourage, and comfort. Words that help propel others into their God-given destinies.

Our church in Toufen is a prophetic church. (Wish I could take credit for that.) Through the years, we've learned to tune into what God is desiring to say to those around us. Almost every time we pray for someone, they'll receive a prophetic encouragement. "I think God wants you to know ..." "I just saw this picture in my mind that I believe is for you ..." These words don't come from our own hearts like the encouraging words we focused on in chapter 15. These words come from God.

Almost every Sunday, a pastor will call one or two believers up front to prophesy over the rest of the congregation. It might be a word that applies to all of us. Or it might be a word given to a specific person that God has highlighted. Or it might be a word given to a group of people in the room, determined by God's specific directions. "Will everyone wearing a red scarf please stand up?" Yes, it takes humility and boldness. But our guys are getting better and better at using this honor-enhancing tool.

We've also tapped into the power of prophetic art. Every week, one or two church members will paint a picture that's based on a prophetic word they feel God has given them. Amazing how often God uses these paintings to make a personal impact. There have been two instances where I was scheduled to preach my sermon (my diligently prepared sermon) but God had other plans. Just as our worship time ended, I felt Him say, "Put away your notes, Gregg. Today, you're going to speak from the prophetic painting in front of you." This was five minutes before I preached! The congregation, of course, was delighted. Because they knew this meant a shorter sermon. A much shorter sermon. But I know that both times, God spoke powerfully through my digging into the prophetic message that saturated these paintings.

Just about every year, we'll take many of these prophetic paintings and turn them into postcard-sized pieces of art. Tools we've learned to use in prophesying over those around us. When Eva and I go back to the U.S. or Denmark, she will carry a bunch of these cards with her. While we're out visiting a family member or friend, she'll ask God to show her which pic He wants to use to speak over their life. Powerful prophecy made easier. Eva's also been known to use these prophetic art cards to release individual encouragement in small groups or meetings. This has the hugely added benefit of other people being able to hear her specific prophetic words spoken over each individual. Which helps establish a local culture of honor. When they hear Eva speak God's value over the different recipients, they begin to gain a new, higher perspective. They begin to view those around them with fresh eyes. His eyes.

So, go prophesy! But first, a quick word of caution. Before jumping in feet first, you should probably get some training. There are, believe it or not, more than a few ways to create a mess if you don't know what you're doing. (Like prophesying to a couple with fertility issues that they'll get pregnant in two months. Or declaring to a single woman that she'll get married by the end of the year. Or announcing to a businessman that God wants him to sell his business and become a missionary to India.) A bit of training is definitely in order! Go read some good books about prophecy. (*They May All Prophesy* by Steve Thompson comes to mind.) Go attend some good workshops or seminars. (Bethel Church in Redding, California comes to mind.) And then, by all means, go prophesy!

As I already mentioned, heart-level encouragement is hugely important. But genuine prophecy even more so. It touches deeper, impacts more powerfully, and transforms more thoroughly. All because it comes straight from the Throne Room. I encourage you, go tap into His throne and water those around you. You'll be amazed by what comes sprouting out of the ground. You'll stand in awe at what this kind of honor produces.

GOLD GOSSIP

We all understand the dangers of gossip, don't we? Credit a lot of that to the much-beloved feather illustration. Seems that several hundred years ago, a woman approached her priest, St. Philip Neri, feeling guilty about her tendency to gossip. (That ugly habit of saying negative things about others behind their backs.) She asked if there was anything at all she could do to make up for her sin. The priest answered, "No problem! Meet me tomorrow morning at the top of the city's bell tower with a feather pillow." The expected act of penance sounded pretty easy so far.

The next morning, they both showed up at the top of the tower, the priest standing quietly by, the woman with pillow in hand. St. Neri then instructed her to rip open the pillow and toss the feathers down all over the city. Not such a hard task, what with the wind doing most of the work. But just then, the priest looked over at the woman and said, "Now here's what I want you to do. Go out and collect every one of those feathers you just released over the people of our city. Every single one." She gasped, of course, at the enormity of the task. And suddenly got the point. Gossip is easy to deliver but nearly impossible to clean up.

There are six clear instances in the New Testament epistles where we are warned about the sin of gossip. Three of those times are kind of repetitious. Something like, "Don't be malicious gossips!" "Don't be malicious gossips!" "Don't be malicious gossips!" (I Timothy 3, II Timothy 3, and Titus 2) Something you might find intriguing here is that the Greek word for gossip in these three verses is *diabolos*. That's right. Very same word used for the "devil." Our false accuser. (Go let that one knock around in your noodle for a bit.) Gossip accuses. Gossip dishonors. Gossip devalues. Pretty devilish stuff.

But before going too far down that negative "Don't! Don't! Don't!" brick road, I'd like to suggest we switch things up a bit. There's a better, more kingdom way to use the inherent power of gossip. Instead of dishing dirt about others behind their backs, let's learn to dish gold about them behind their backs. Let's make a Jesus-sanctioned commitment to spread positive reports rather than negative. Words of affirmation, honor, and value as opposed to devilish accusations.

This is a lot easier to do than you might think.

First, choose your target. Maybe someone at church or work or even a family member who's a bit of an outsider. Doesn't seem to fit in. Or one of the forgotten or neglected or lonely in your social circles. Or one of the too-shy kind who struggles with identity issues. Or maybe even one of the already branded bad guys hanging around the fringes. Name firmly affixed to the rotten reputation, no-respect list. You get the idea. Go find your target.

Then grab your feather pillow. Brainstorm several positive things about this person that other people might not know. Hidden talents, acts of service, character qualities, passions, or special attitudes you've noticed. Any gold feather qualifies.

Then go find your bell tower. That place where you plan to release the feathers one at a time. Could be your church coffee bar, or in a business meeting at work, or around your family dinner table, or at your weekly knitting club, or in the teacher's lounge at school. You just need people around, even one will do, to hear the positive gossip you can't wait to share.

Then rip and release. Just one little feather to start things off. (Because you don't want to freak people out with a huge feather overload at once.)

"Did you ever notice how responsible Andy is when he serves in the church coffee bar? First one in, last one out." That's it. No five-minute explanation needed. One feather at a time.

"Mary's such a fantastic mother. She's so patient with her children."

"Can you believe the worship gifting that Kevin carries? What a blessing to us all!"

"Nora's attention to detail has saved us so many times though the years. Off the charts amazing!"

"Bobby, I just love your new teacher at school! She's so creative!"

All done behind Andy's back, Mary's back, Kevin's back, Nora's back, and the new teacher's back. Because that's how gold gossip is done. I encourage you to enlist the help of your kingdom-focused brothers and sisters. And pretty soon, propelled by the wind of the Spirit, gold feathers will begin to impact your communities. Church, family, work, school, and knitting club.

A fresh culture of honor will rise up. Others will begin to look at your gold gossip targets in a new light, opening the door to treating them with greater value. Which will eventually change the way your precious targets view themselves. Which, of course, is the whole goal of honor.

One feather at a time, spoken in the right place at the right moment to the right people, can be explosive. The good kind of explosive. So go let that gold gossip fly!

CHAPTER SIXTEEN

WITHOUT WORDS

❦

G ot a couple of quick questions for you. Who do you most enjoy hanging out with and why? I'm not talking about your golf buddies or movie buddies or video game buddies or museum-hopping buddies. I'm thinking more along the lines of coffee buddies or couch buddies. People you really like to chat with. So, one more time, who are your favorite chat buddies and why?

I'm guessing most of you enjoy hanging out with people who hang on your every word. They lean forward, ask good questions, and genuinely listen to what you have to say. Both ears wide open. And you can feel it, can't you? You feel cared for. You feel special. You feel valuable. You feel listened to. Don't you just love being around people like that?

We've been looking at some of the kinds of words we can speak that sow seeds of honor in another person's heart. Encouraging words, empowering words, and prophetic words. All value-building words. But sometimes, not speaking can actually have a huge honor impact. And I'm not just talking about having the self-discipline to close your mouth before dishonoring words come gushing out. The act of genuine listening is often more powerful than we could ever imagine.

In 2008, I underwent extensive radiation therapy for advanced cancer. That meant eight weeks of daily sessions in "the machine." I was given an assigned time to show up every day, put on my lovely gown, and wait in the freezing hallway for my name to be called. And I wasn't the only one waiting. My fellow radiation buddies with similar time slots were also there. Always there. I especially remember one elderly gentleman. At times he sat next to me, and boy, did we have some great conversations. Only problem was, I didn't understand a word he said. He only spoke the Taiwanese dialect, while I knew basic Mandarin, a smattering of the Hakka dialect, and only three words of his Taiwanese tongue. (One of which is not very polite.) So my new friend would talk. And I would sit next to him nodding, smiling when it seemed appropriate, and expressing interest in what he had to say.

On the day of my final treatment, Eva came along and started up a conversation with my radiation buddy's wife. Afterwards, as we were driving home, she told me that this elderly gentleman's wife was so appreciative of how I encouraged her husband through our time together. He'd been going through a fairly depressing season, and apparently I told him just the things he needed to hear. Amazing man that I am. Who couldn't understand a lick of what this precious man said, and didn't utter a meaningful word the entire time.

But here's the deal. Even though I didn't understand this man, he felt heard. He felt cared for, valuable, and honored. That alone, by God's miraculous grace, had a remarkable impact on my hospital friend, helping to deliver him from his radiation funk. Imagine how effective genuine real-deal listening can be. In God's "honor all people" armory, there is no more powerful weapon.

Here are a couple of thoughts to chew on before you lock and load.

Great listening takes a bit of planning. Off the cuff is great, and necessary at times, but doesn't always make it out the gate. So be intentional. Invite your target of honor to join you somewhere for a good cup-of-hot-something. (Emphasis on the invite and the where, not the hot-something.) And then, long before you jump in the car, start preparing your heart to be a great listener. Think about the other person. Focus on them. Seek God's heart and insights. And come up with a list of good questions that show your interest in them. Who they are, how they're doing, what they've been doing, and what hopes, desires, fears, or worries they carry.

As you finally sit across from your target of honor, enjoying your cup-of-hot-something and asking your thoughtfully prepared questions, make sure you continue to focus on listening to them. Really listening. It's so easy to hear what they're saying and slip in your own "I had something like that happen to me once" interjection. Equally tempting is the desire to impart a few bits of "much-needed" advice. At the risk of riding the rude, shut that thinking down! It's not about you, so please don't make it about you. Follow up their answers by asking even deeper questions, trying to understand them better or helping them to discover treasure they've never seen before.

One final tip, and it's a biggie. Genuine listening involves the whole body, not just the ears and the brain. Years ago, I was a pastor-of-sorts at a missionary training base in Hawaii. One day, I ran into a serious problem I had no idea how to deal with. So, I headed off to see my leader. To share my angst about the issue and to hear if he thought my possible solutions were on track or not. This leader, a wonderful, godly guy, invited me into his house and showed me to the couch. He sat down in a chair across from me and I started sharing. I didn't get two minutes in before he suddenly stood up and walked over to the front door. I paused for a second, but he motioned that I should continue. So I did. And he started using his thumb to kill a long line of ants, one at a time, that were marching down his door and into his house. My heart sank. I felt he hadn't heard a word I'd been saying. And that the ants were more important than me or my problem. I weakly finished whatever conversation we'd had, and made my exit. Not an ounce of feeling cared for, listened to, valued, or honored.

So, make sure your body lines up with your focused-on-them mindset. Hide your cell phone, lean slightly forward, make eye contact, nod to express understanding, and smile when appropriate. But please, please, please, even if you feel like you have this amazing gift to do two things at once, don't ever get up from your chair and kill the line of ants marching into your house. Ever. (Did I mention hiding your cell phone? Turning it off? Ignoring it when it dings? Not glancing over at it no matter what dance it does?) Don't focus on the ants parading down the door! There are more important things sitting in front of you. Waiting to be heard. Waiting to be cared for. Waiting to be honored.

Genuine listening is a powerful weapon! Make sure and use it to honor those around you.

A GLIMPSE OF HONOR
CASTING THE NET
❧

I t started one night near the end of February, 2022. Someone in our Toufen church formed a special group of brothers and sisters, the "153 Club," to lift up me and Eva. Based on the number of fish caught by Jesus' disciples when He told them where to let down their nets, (John 21:11) the purpose of this special club was to cast a giant net around our lives, aiming for a great catch of encouragement, support, and healing.

I heard from Eva that a few people had come to pray for us. But as I was led down the stairs and through our garage to the ground level, I began to suspect we'd been set up. The sound of voices got louder and louder, and as the garage door opened, Eva and I were met by a mob of about thirty angels from the church, waiting with special anticipation for us to take our special seats of honor. Then the cheerleading, chanting, and loud music cranked up. And all these wonderful, crazy people, young and old alike, started a choreographed dance number that would have qualified for America's Got Talent. It was wild, full of energy, and put huge smiles on our faces.

At the end of their five-minute song and dance, everyone from the 153 Club gathered around to pray and prophesy over us. A huge 5x3 foot canvas with a gorgeous tree painted on it was affixed to the wall just outside our garage door, heavy gold string stretching across the top in several places. (With a stack of notecards, pens, and tiny colored clothes pins piled up neatly nearby.)

One of the leaders came forward and told Eva and me that the goal of their club was to pray for and encourage us until God called them to stop. Could be two days. Could be two weeks. Only God knew. Every single day after this first dance party, someone showed up in front of our house and prayed for us. And left a short prophetic note, encouragement, drawing, or Bible verse hanging on the painting of the giant tree. More than a few times, I'd walk through our living room and hear the sound of several members of the "153 Club" outside praying for us. But that's not all. Almost daily, someone would come by and leave us special snacks, meals, small gifts, or generous donations in a special "Drop-Off Drawer" hidden under the staircase. It was intense. And relentless. And we loved it.

Two months later, the leaders of the group felt God was calling them to end this special prayer, prophecy, joy, hope, and peace bombardment. You read right. Each and every day for two months, the angels of the "153 Club" came by our house and cast their precious nets around our lives.

This is what kingdom honor looks like. Bestowing God's value on those in its crosshairs.

CHAPTER SEVENTEEN
THE DIVINE DAZER
c~oc~o

J esus got dissed and His disciples got pissed. On their final journey to Jerusalem, Jesus sent messengers into a Samaritan village to make lodging arrangements for the night. (Luke 9) When the villagers found out the Jews were headed for Jerusalem, these half-breeds refused to receive them. Thus the dissing. Of Jesus. Son of God. The Messiah.

As expected, the sons of thunder were furious. With just the right amount of holy indignation, and thoughts of Elijah dancing in their heads, James and John asked Jesus if He wanted them to call down fire from heaven and obliterate the whole offensive village. Turning sharply to the brothers, the dissed One rebuked them. (With just the right amount of holy indignation.) "You don't understand what kind of spirit you're responding in! It's certainly not mine, because I didn't come to destroy men's lives, but to save them!"

We have within our hearts the capacity to respond from either an offended spirit or a gracious spirit. To speak words of death or words of life. To tear down or build up. To humiliate or honor. To stone or enthrone. Sometimes the choice doesn't always come easy.

When I was in Junior High School, I had the reputation of being a nice kid. A really nice kid. In fact, at the end of seventh grade, I was the sole recipient of the Ward Simmons Courtesy Award. (Hoozah!) What few people know is that it almost didn't happen.

In gym class, earlier that same year, we were playing an indoor football-type of game. With time running out, I caught the football for a game-winning score. Just as I crossed the goal line, someone from the losing team shoved me hard into the wall and I crumpled to the ground, stunned. Looking back, I saw the class bully in full retreat. Filled with a rage I'd never experienced before, I jumped up and started running after the evil tyrant, ready to deposit some payback. (That's right, the nicest, most polite kid in the seventh grade was racing to beat up one of his fellow-students. He was bigger, but I had rage on my side.) Two of my friends, names lost to me now, saw what had happened, saw what was about to happen, and saw the look on my face. They heroically jumped in and held me back from attacking the young man who'd shoved me into the wall. If it weren't for these two friends, I never would have won the coveted Courtesy Award at the end of the year. Nicest kid in the class.

Chances are, you seldom face situations where a class bully brutally shoves you into a wall. But how many times have others brutally shoved you into a metaphoric wall with their very real words? Harsh words. Belittling words. Rejecting words. Shaming words. Accusing words. The bullies usually coming in the form of a boss, co-worker, spouse, parent, or teacher. The big question, of course, is how you responded to the wall-shove. Did you get angry, jump off the floor, and start wailing away on the offender? Did you lash out with your own bully certified words trying to hurt the person who hurt you?

Proverbs 16:32 says that "he who is slow to anger is better than the mighty, and he who rules his spirit, than he who captures a city." When you are able to rule your spirit, you are more powerful than any conquering king. When you are able to control your anger or frustration or jealousy or disappointment or sense of loss, you can walk through life in victory. Dispensing words of life instead of words of death.

So, what's the big secret? How can you successfully rule your spirit? Let's start with Galatians 5:22-23. The fruits of the Spirit listed here are (by obvious definition) things produced in your life when you are filled with God's Spirit. Notice that the last fruit mentioned is self-control. Being master over your own desires and impulses. Also known as ruling your spirit. Isn't it interesting that self-control comes from being under the control of the Holy Spirit? (This is the kind of thing that keeps me awake at night!) So, just who does this work of self-control in your life? You or the Holy Spirit? Both, of course. Working together in a powerful partnership to make sure you can successfully rule your spirit. You do your part, and the Spirit helps you do your part. (Sorry, but I feel like I have to repeat that.) You do your part, and the Spirit helps you do your part.

Some years ago, on my daily walks, I passed by a house located on a very narrow backstreet—and an adjoining doghouse within spitting distance. Every day I walked down that street, a huge, chained-up dog would jump out and scare the living daylights out of me. Every single day. It was like sport to him. For the sake of my heart, I decided to do something about this hound from hell. A few years earlier, I'd bought something called a Dazer. When the button on this handheld device was pressed, a silent (to humans) sound was emitted, scaring away any overly aggressive dogs. This was going to be the key to my victory.

One day, Dazer in hand, I went on my usual walk. As I neared the doghouse, I sensed the huge dog watching and waiting, delighted with the opportunity to leap out and scare me again. But this time I was ready. Just as the dog made his move, I hit the Dazer button. What a difference! He immediately stopped barking and sulked back to the safety of his doghouse, not quite sure what had hit him. This continued for the next week. Every day, the same routine. Every day, the same lying in wait, lunging and barking. Every day, the same Dazer defense. Every day, the same confused sulk back to the doghouse.

And then, at the end of the week, something changed. As I approached the house that day, the dog saw me coming. I could almost hear him thinking, "Should I jump out and scare this guy today?" After a moment's pause, his ears went down and he walked slowly back to his doghouse. Defeated. I never used the Dazer again, and he never charged out and scared me again.

Yes, this has a point. Every morning, I encourage you to ask the Holy Spirit to use His Dazer on you whenever you're in danger of jumping out and barking at someone. "Holy Spirit, use your Dazer on me when I need it. Set a guard over my heart. Set a guard over my emotions. Set a guard over my words. Set a guard over my actions. Get my attention, shake me awake, lovingly zap my conscience when You see me beginning to respond in the wrong spirit." Believe me, the Holy Spirit loves answering this prayer. He loves using His divine Dazer to train you to rule your spirit. And He longs for the day when you won't need to be zapped anymore because your heart has been transformed.

From sowing death to sowing life. From tearing down to building up. From stoning to enthroning. Rising up in your kingdom call to honor all people.

CHAPTER EIGHTEEN

THE KORAH CONUNDRUM

e⌒∞⌒⁹

A s mentioned earlier, some people are harder to honor than others. In the same way, some kinds of relationships struggle more than others to foster a culture of honor. Probably the most challenging of these, the ones we need to keep closest watch over, are the roles of leading and following. Being in authority and being submitted to authority. Boss, employee. Parent, child. Teacher, student. Pastor, church member. Husband, wife. See any potential for dishonor in these kinds of relationships?

When I was 23-years old, fresh out of college with a degree in business, I was hired to be the manager of a travel agency. Pretty impressive, huh? Hired on the spot. Without ever having to submit a resume or sit for an interview. Wealth of managerial experience? (I was 23!) Stellar grades in college? (Wish I could insert a smiley face here.) Truth is, my dad owned the agency.

It took me a few months to get settled in. I went to the required training, observed how things worked out front with the customers and in back with the bookkeeper. Got to know all the travel agents under my care. All the while, trying to figure out how to turn around a failing business. After about six months of doing my management thing, I decided we needed a little change out front, where all the ladies did their agent thing. Not much. Just move a couple of desks around to make things more customer-friendly.

I explained the whats and whys of my changes to the agents, and after everyone left for the night, I got started. Moved the two desks. Tidied things up. Looked forward to how my charges would react when they saw it. Imagine my surprise when I arrived the next morning and found one of the desks moved back to its original place. I called the agent of said desk into my office and asked this mid-fiftiesh woman why she'd changed it back. Seems she thought the desk belonged to her and that she could do with it what she darn well pleased. I was stunned. Employees weren't supposed to respond that way to their bosses. At least, not in my young, starry-eyed view of the world. After explaining, more clearly this time, what we were doing with the office, I went back out and relocated her desk. The next morning, I walked in the front door and saw that the desk fairies had been at work again. Oh joy. My next talk was more unpleasant. She threatened to quit, and I didn't stand in her way.

Then and there, I began to learn that this authority dynamic can be dead tough to navigate. The roles of leading and following carry the kind of baggage that can present a huge challenge to walking in Jesus-style honor. Which is why we're going to take a good, close look at them both.

The best place to begin is understanding that these two roles are designed and created by God. They were His idea from the very beginning. Authority is His idea, and submission is His idea. The Bible, Genesis to Revelation, is packed with teaching after teaching, example after example, of how God has called us to function rightly in these two crucial responsibilities.

So, why the struggle? Why such angst when trying to walk godly in these two roles? Because many of us have bought into the world's thinking that leaders are more valuable than followers, and followers are less valuable than leaders. (Tell me I'm wrong.) Jesus would never think this way, and neither should we. Those who lead and those who follow are equally important in His eyes. If we don't fully understand or believe these truths, insecurity will likely creep into our hearts. And insecurity gives birth to harsh, bullying, or manipulative leaders, and disgruntled, rebellious, or dispirited followers.

Remember Korah and his band of 250 misguided rebels? Well-respected leaders in their own right, they approached Moses and Aaron in the wilderness and demanded the top spot. As you might recall, God was not pleased. The earth opened up and swallowed Korah and three of his cohorts, while fire from heaven fell down and devoured the other 250. Ouch. But most telling is the sad reason they launched the rebellion, witnessed by the words they spoke when approaching Moses and Aaron. "Why do you think you're so much better than anyone else? We're part of the Lord's holy people, and He's with all of us." (Numbers 16:3, CEV) Did you hear it? "Why do you think you're more valuable, more important than us?! We're valuable too! We're important too!" Like I said, sad. They thought higher leadership would bestow a higher value on them. They thought wrong. Because leadership is a role, a function, a responsibility, not a gauge of true value. Wonder how many of us have adopted the corrupted thinking of this world and believe the same thing Korah did. Like I said, sad.

With this truth in place, the next two chapters are going to focus on how to be an honoring leader and an honoring follower. Things that can help guard these tough to navigate relationships in our lives.

CHAPTER NINETEEN
WAITING TABLES
❧

Attention all CEOs, schoolteachers, pastors, moms and dads, mid-level managers, worship team leaders, athletic coaches, husbands, small business owners, university professors, home group leaders, military officers, mayors, medical doctors, or any other of the countless varieties of leaders in life: This chapter is for you!

The world's approach to leadership has been around for a very long time. Just ask Jesus. His own followers were having a long-running dispute about which of them was most qualified to be the top dog in the coming kingdom. Which of them had the right stuff to sit in that coveted place of power and authority. Which of them was the greatest. (See Luke 22:24-27.)

Jesus reclined at the table, taking in their back and forth. (Yes, that table. In the upper room. During Passover week. Just hours before the Lamb would be sacrificed.) He finally stilled the debate with a startling declaration. "The leaders of this world lord it over those under their rule, using their authority as a weapon to control the people. All the while trying to come across as selfless, compassionate do-gooders. Of the people and for the people! But you guys are not to be like this. You are not to think or act like the world. My kingdom way is radically different. The greatest among you should be like the youngest, like the very least. And whoever is given authority to rule should be like the one who serves. Tell Me this, who is greater, the person who reclines at the table or the one who serves him? It's obviously the one who reclines at the table being served. Well, get this. I am here living among you as the One who serves. The One who waits tables. The Creator God, King of kings, Lord of lords, Son of God, promised Messiah, Savior of the world, has been sent from heaven to earth to be your servant." (I wouldn't doubt for a second that this was when He got up from the table and washed His disciples' feet.)

Jesus' revelation of kingdom leadership in these few verses is absolutely mind-blowing. And tells those of you in authority just about everything you need to know about how to be a powerful, successful, honoring leader. I know, I know. There are stacks and stacks of incredible books, sermons, and podcasts on how to lead like Jesus. Countless leadership keys, principles, values, habits, and strategies. I encourage you, go read these books. Go listen to all the sermons and podcasts you can. But understand this: Jesus' one-point sermon here in Luke 22 is the only place to start. Because everything else flows from it.

If you want to be an honoring leader, you need to serve the ones you lead.

As Jesus pointed out, the world's way of leadership is all about lording it over the ones you're leading. By whatever means possible. Threats, pressure, shame, competition, comparison, anger, manipulation, disapproval, or disgust. Like a valuable patron in a fancy restaurant might treat his lowly server. Barking out orders, showing no tolerance for mistakes, making little or no eye contact, not caring a whit about who they are or what they're going through in life, and leaving absurdly low tips.

Jesus flips the table on the world's ways. Your main job as a kingdom leader is to get up from the table (just like Jesus did), place those under your care in seats of honor, and serve them hand and foot. (Luke 22:27) Even writing these words seems crazy, but Jesus would never call us to do something He didn't do. In Matthew 20:28, He says this about Himself. "... the Son of Man did not come to be served, but to serve, and to give His life a ransom for many." Every leader should have this posted on his or her bathroom mirror.

Leading with honor means you do "not come to be served, but to serve." Which means it's not about you, it's about them. You are called to help those you lead to succeed in what God has called them to do. To help them grow in character. To help blossom their gifts and talents. To give them opportunities for advancement. To give them favor with others who can prosper them on their journey. To care for them, encourage them, love them, and empower them. To help them see and reach the destiny God has for their lives.

And to make sure they understand just how valuable they are in His eyes. Because that's what honor is all about.

CEOs, this is for you. Schoolteachers, this is for you. Pastors, this is for you. Moms and dads, this is for you. Mid-level managers, this is for you. Ministry team leaders, this is for you. Small business owners, this is for you. Husbands, this is for you.

Remember my story in the last chapter about managing a travel agency when I was 23? And the employee who rebelled against my leadership because she thought the desk belonged to her? And my forcing her to either submit or quit? Oh, that I would have known then what I know now about Jesus-style leadership. Oh, that I would have been more patient and caring. Oh, that I would have taken the time to get to know her better. Oh, that I would have been more sensitive to her thoughts and feelings. Oh, that I would have seen it as my mission to encourage and edify and empower her. Oh, that I would have been more concerned about her destiny than my own. Oh, that I would have valued her the way Jesus did. Oh, that I would have gotten up from the table, seated her in a place of honor, and served her hand and foot. So many years later, I wonder how things would have turned out.

I told you in chapter seven that I believe the best definition of honor in the Bible is found in Philippians 2:3-7. It's also the best picture of kingdom leadership in the Bible, describing the greatest leader our universe has ever seen. I encourage you to read this slowly and thoughtfully, through the eyes of a leader. (And since your bathroom mirror is already booked, I recommend attaching this to your refrigerator door.)

"Do nothing from selfishness or empty conceit, but with humility of mind regard [the ones you lead] as more important than yourselves; do not merely look out for your own personal interests, but also for the interests of [these precious ones under your care]. Have this attitude in yourselves which was also in Christ Jesus, who, although He existed in the form of God, did not regard equality with God a thing to be grasped, but emptied Himself, taking the form of a bond-servant, and being made in the likeness of men."

He rose from the table, laid aside his clothes, wrapped a towel around His waist, and served those who were seated in His places of honor. The twelve. His beloved disciples. Those who had just moments earlier been arguing about which of them was the most important, the most valuable, the greatest.

Jesus ended the debate. Showing all of them, and us, what true greatness looks like.

CHAPTER TWENTY
HOMETOWN WELL WATER
❧

A ttention all government workers, factory workers, ministry team members, children still living at
home, church staff, nursing staff, maintenance staff,
office staff, wives, mid-level managers, associate pastors,
restaurant workers, Walmart workers, church members, UPS
drivers, lawn care laborers, and any one of a million other
positions in life where you are submitted to some kind of
authority: This chapter is for you!

The idea of obeying (following) the leaders in your life
should be fairly straightforward. The Bible is chock full of
admonitions and examples that give us a good picture. It goes
something like this. "Don't rebel. Submit to your leaders. Do
what they tell you to do."

Eva and I used to have a dog named Lester who was part
Shiba Inu, a Japanese breed known as the "cat dog." Maybe
because of their ability to climb trees, maybe because of their

stubborn independence. Now, Lester was a very smart dog (said the proud owner), learning quickly to sit on command. "Lester, sit!" Troubling thing is, she refused to go all the way to the ground. Serious obedience issues. Serious spirit of rebellion. Serious submission concerns. For fourteen years, every time we commanded her to sit, she'd go through the right motions, but her butt—the most important part of sitting—always remained a couple inches off the ground. Always.

Don't have to spell this one out, do I? The most goes-without-saying part of following with honor is submitting wholeheartedly to your leaders. If they tell you to sit, submit. Not a Lester sit, but a full-on, butt-all-the-way-to-the-ground kind of sit. Unless your leaders ask you to do something that's against the will or ways of God, obey them. With joy. This is the most essential requirement for Jesus-style submission to authority. The author of Hebrews 13:17 framed it like this. "Obey your leaders and submit to them, for they keep watch over your souls as those who will give an account. Let them do this with joy and not with grief, for this would be unprofitable for you." Easy peasy. Unless you happen to be like Lester.

But I'm not just going for the easy peasy in this chapter. There's a whole different level of following with honor that I would like you to see and embrace. Something that can release huge doses of peace, joy, and hope into this usually tough to navigate relationship.

Sometime before David became king, probably while he was still running from Saul, he and his faithful band of warriors found themselves near the cave of Adullam. Which was within spitting distance of David's hometown of Bethlehem. One day, the future king found himself getting a bit homesick,

pining for something, anything, that would satisfy his longing for home. A longing that seemed impossible because his
hometown was now swarming with Philistine stormtroopers.

Thinking no one else was around, David sighed, "Oh
that someone would give me water to drink from the well
of Bethlehem!" Three of his mighty men were close enough
to hear his sighed desires. They immediately raced down to
Bethlehem, unsheathed their weapons, broke through the
camp of the enemy, drew water from the hometown well,
and took it straight back to David. Who was astonished. And
humbled. And honored. The devotion shown by these three
warriors, risking their lives to bring David his heart's desire,
was so extravagant, so costly, that he poured the water out
on the ground as a holy sacrifice to God. Their honor was
far, far more valuable than a drink from his hometown well.
They had submitted to his deep longings, not just his spoken commands.

What a great picture for us as followers! Let's get close
to our leaders, hear their hearts' desires, and do everything
we can to see these longings fulfilled. No matter the cost.
That's what Jesus-style submission is all about.

I've got another story in my pocket, one of my favorites.
And absolutely unbelievable.

King Saul's army was bogged down in war with the
Philistines, but there wasn't much fighting going on. One day,
the king's son, Jonathan, said to his armor bearer, "Let's cross
over the valley to the stronghold of these ungodly Philistines.
Maybe the Lord will do a great work through the two of us,
because He is able to give victory no matter how many or few

we are." The young man said to Jonathan, "Do all that is in your heart; turn yourself, and here I am with you according to your desire." (I Samuel 14:7) Are you beginning to hear the unbelievable part yet?

Jonathan and his armor bearer then crossed the valley and stood looking up the steep cliff where the Philistines were camped. The enemy soldiers saw the two Israelites and called out, inviting them to climb up for a visit. So, in the face of ridiculous odds, Jonathan and the young man crawled up the cliff on their hands and knees, reached the top, and slaughtered the entire camp. Because God was with them. Their miraculous victory that day echoed all the way back to Saul's camp and resulted in even mightier victories for the whole Israelite army.

Don't you just love Jonathan's armor bearer? Has there ever been a better example of what it looks like to follow with honor? When his leader, Jonathan, suggested they do something crazy, something that could get them killed, he said, "Do everything that's in your heart! I'm with you all the way!" (Unbelievable!) He was fully committed to doing whatever he could to help his master succeed. To help him accomplish his heart's desire.

Ministry team members, this is for you. Factory workers, this is for you. Church staff, this is for you. Nursing staff, this is for you. Walmart workers, this is for you. Restaurant workers, this is for you. Wives, this is for you.

Kingdom submission is more than simple submission. More than just obeying what you're told to do. It's learning what deep desires reside in your leader's heart and doing whatever you can to help these longings get fulfilled. To help them accomplish their dreams and aspirations. To help them get a drink from their hometown well. To have the same attitude as Jonathan's armor bearer. "Do everything that's in your heart! I'm with you all the way!" Make it your main aim as a follower to show your leaders just how valuable they are to you.

Because that's what unbelievable honor is all about.

A GLIMPSE OF HONOR
HELLO DARKNESS

I n 1961, when Sanford Greenberg[5] was a junior at Columbia University, he went completely blind. Sitting at home with a no-hope diagnosis, Sanford gave up all ideas of getting his degree or doing anything important with his life. Then his college roommate, Arthur, showed up.

One of the first things he did was insist that Sanford was going to return to the university and finish his studies. And that he, Arthur, was going to help him do it. They argued back and forth, Sanford pointing out that his friend could only help him at the expense of his own studies. He simply didn't have the time or energy to help his blind roommate while pursuing his own degree in architecture.

---

5 Sandford D. Greenberg, *Hello Darkness, My Old Friend* (Post Hill Press, June 6, 2022)

When Arthur asked him what he wanted in life, Sanford's somewhat self-pitying reply was, "Just give me one more day in the sunshine, Arthur. That's all I ask." Just one more day to see again. But Arthur dismissed the self-pity. And the hopeless response. "You've already lived a fine life, Sanford, and I think yours will be a long life. No, you won't see the sun, but the fire in you will lead you to achievements that others can only dream about. Listen to me, Sanford. You will be a great man, a hero. Greatness will be yours."

So they returned to the university. Together. And Arthur served his blind friend, just like he'd promised, helping in every way possible to make sure Sanford succeeded. He led him by elbow around campus, the city streets, and the subway stations. Anywhere he needed to go. He bandaged the nicks, cuts, and bruises from all the falls and rogue lampposts. But most of all, Arthur read and read and read to Sanford. Everything. From lecture notes, to countless chapters in countless textbooks, to teachers' assignments and comments, to stacks of newspapers and ordinary mail. According to Sanford, "There was nothing he would not do for me." And sometimes, on those late night reading sessions, Arthur would begin by simply saying, "Darkness is going to help you today." A beautiful picture that his voice, Arthur's voice, was now emerging from the darkness to be his friend.

And it worked. With Arthur's help and encouragement, Sanford became president of his class and graduated Phi Beta Kappa. On time. He would go on to become an author, inventor, public servant, and philanthropist. He launched two successful technology firms, was a longstanding member of the U.S. Council on Foreign Relations, and in 2016, was inducted into the American Academy of Arts and Sciences.

Though Arthur would eventually get a bachelor's degree in art history and a master's in mathematics education, he never became an architect. Instead, he became a singer. Art Garfunkel. Of Simon and Garfunkel fame. "Hello darkness, my old friend."

Such a remarkable picture of genuine honor at work.

CHAPTER TWENTY-ONE
TOUGH LOVE HONOR
❧

If you remember, I kicked off this book with the familiar story of Jesus and the woman caught in adultery. (John 8) Like most tellings of the tale, mine showed just enough nuance to make the point I wanted to make, but not enough to reveal the full story. And this story needs more nuance. It wasn't just a powerful display of Jesus saving this adulteress from the harsh, finger-pointing, stone-throwing Pharisees. And it wasn't just a beautiful example of setting her free through His gentle brand of condemnation-free grace. There was so much more going on here. A tough love kind of honor which extended to just about everyone within earshot.

This poor woman was actually caught in the act of adultery. She either cheated on her own husband or was trying to steal another woman's husband. Or both. Not nice. With the very likely consequence of destroying two families. When Jesus set her free with His grace-filled, "Woman, did no one condemn you? Then neither do I," He then valued her enough to command her to stop sinning. And He valued the involved families enough to command her to stop sinning. The only One qualified to throw the first stone didn't throw it, but He did give her some tough love honor. "Go. From now on sin no more." In other words, "Stop it!" An act of honor that served to protect this woman (and both families) from her destructive, sinful actions.

And let's not forget the harsh, finger-pointing, stone-throwing Pharisees. Jesus didn't respond to them in the same harsh, dishonoring manner they treated the woman with. He didn't jump up in righteous anger, read them the riot act, start shaming them one by one, name by name, for their own sins, revealing the hidden secrets of their filthy hearts. He could have. I sure might have been tempted to. But Jesus saw the God-given value in these men. So He settled the situation down and gave them time to work it out for themselves. (While writing on the ground.)

And notice the tough love honor He showed when He stood back up and nudged them in the right direction with, "He who is without sin among you, let him be the first to throw a stone." (And stooped down again, giving them even more time to reach their own conclusions. Which they finally did.) Do you see it? Jesus valued these men enough to protect them from their blind, self-righteous ways. And to protect those in the path of their blind, self-righteous ways. That's a whole lot of honor going on. Tough love honor.

I was hesitant to put this chapter in the book. Mostly because I know that some of you might be tempted to use this "tough love honor" idea as an excuse to put on your sin-hunter hats and confront those who cross the line. I get it. I'm a black and white, right or wrong kind of guy myself, naturally leaning toward judgment instead of grace. Sadly, I would probably have made a great finger pointing Pharisee. If you tend to live in this same camp, please approach these thoughts with care. I sure do.

Sometimes, genuine kingdom honor demands confrontation. In Galatians 6:1, Paul wrote, "Dear brothers and sisters, if another believer is overcome by some sin, you who are godly should gently and humbly help that person back onto the right path." (NLT) Hear the honor in that kind of confrontation? The focus is not on policing the sin, but on restoring the kingdom value and destiny of the fallen one.

And the epistle penned by James ends with these two powerful verses. "My dear brothers and sisters, if someone among you wanders away from the truth and is brought back, you can be sure that whoever brings the sinner back from wandering will save that person from death and bring about the forgiveness of many sins." (NLT) The goals of this kind of confrontation are so, so clear. To save the wanderer from his wandering, and to protect the sinner (and those around him) from his sin.

Sometimes, genuine kingdom honor demands confrontation. And to be honest, we don't always do confrontation well. For many of us, the word itself conjures up an in-your-face approach to setting someone straight. It doesn't have to be that way at all. It really shouldn't be that way at all.

Many years ago, I was on staff at a missionary training center in Honolulu, living in a house called Calcutta Mansion with a bunch of other guys. For the most part, we got along great, eating meals together while watching late-afternoon episodes of Knight Rider. But there was one young man who just didn't seem to fit in. Kind of set everyone's teeth on edge a bit. His personal hygiene was atrocious, his manners worse, and he was definitely low on the social etiquette scale. Saying the wrong things at the wrong time, or trying too hard to be liked and accepted.

One day, God spoke clearly to me that I needed to reach out to him. He was getting ready to attend a training school on another island, and from what I'd witnessed, was going to carry all his teeth-on-edge baggage with him. Setting him up for the same struggles he faced with us. I thought God's ask was a big ask. I wasn't one of his leaders and certainly not a close friend, and He wanted me to address some very personal, uncomfortable, boundary-crossing issues.

I ran into the young man later that day while walking across a school field on the way to the local shopping center. Thinking that was as good a time as any, I began by asking if I could talk to him about something a bit awkward, something that might help him fit in better at his upcoming school. As gently as possible, I laid out a few of my thoughts, offering some practical changes he might want to consider. I honestly thought he might be upset, even angry, with my fairly intrusive counsel, but he responded just the opposite. Almost in tears, he thanked me over and over for being open with him, grateful for this honoring confrontation. He'd been so confused all these months about why others didn't seem to like or accept him, and now, a tiny ray of hope opened up as he saw what the problems might be. I was relieved. Elated even.

Especially knowing that God was going to use this to help him fit in better at his new school.

Sometimes, genuine kingdom honor demands confrontation. The one I just mentioned, with no sin involved, was relatively easy, but we all know that some confrontations are far more challenging. Far more open to misunderstanding. Far more open to rejection or hostile responses. Confronting someone about a porn addiction, or lying, or cheating, or gossiping, or committing adultery, or being harsh with others, or anger issues, or ... you get the picture.

Here are a few simple things I've learned through the years that have helped me confront with honor. Things that might help you, as well.

First, make sure you're confronting the person for all the right reasons and none of the wrong. Not because their sin affects or annoys you. Not because you're angry or frustrated with what they're doing and believe there needs to be consequences. Your main goals for the confrontation should be value based. Honor based. Having a passion to see them restored, empowered, set free, and protected. So, instead of focusing on dirt, set your eyes on the gold God sees and adores.

Second, give them the opportunity to be involved in the discovery process. This is far more powerful than dumping your own pre-conceived observations on them. Be like Jesus. Go slow. Ask good questions. Stoop down and write on the ground. Give them a chance to share what they think is going on. Then stoop back down to the ground. Now, they may not come up with the same conclusions, but that's okay. When you give them a safe place of honor in the discovery process, they'll probably be more open to finding and following God's kingdom solutions.

Third, respond in the opposite spirit to any defensive reactions they might fire at you. Receiving correction is rarely easy. No matter how gentle and honoring your approach, you can naturally expect some people to feel threatened and strike back out of deep-seated insecurities. Go into the confrontation prepared to respond to these attacks with humility, love, grace, acceptance, gentleness, and, of course, honor. Because your goal is not winning an argument, but helping the wandering one to walk in genuine freedom and restoration.

Fourth, focus on their God-given value and prophetic destiny. From the very beginning, surround your correction with deep, true, meaningful encouragement. At every appropriate turn, seek to remind them of who they are in God's eyes, and help them get excited about the powerful life He has designed for them. Destiny-based confrontation pumps kingdom hope into their heart, which can result in life-changing restoration.

Sometimes, genuine kingdom honor demands confrontation. The right kind. Done the right way. In the right spirit. For the right results. Valuing others enough to help release them into becoming the world-changers God has called them to be.

CHAPTER TWENTY-TWO
THE DANGER OF A CHICO HEART
೧ᴼᴼ

When I was a teenager, my dad went out and bought a dog for my sister's birthday. A tiny purebred Chihuahua that he quickly christened Chico Choco III. If you know much at all about this south-of-the-border breed, you know they're very special creatures. Ours sure was. As adorable as a cupcake, Chico was also mean as the dickens.

First thing he did when he got home was choose favorites. I was honored with first place in the pecking order. (The birthday girl, two spots below me.) Which meant when we were all sitting around the living room watching T.V., you'd always find Chico curled up next to me. Always. Where he apparently felt the most secure.

Sad thing is, Chico rarely felt safe. His whole life seemed to revolve around fear of those big, threatening things that rose up around him. Which, when you think about it, was pretty much everything. If someone couldn't resist the desire to walk up and pet him, the results were predictable. First, some nervous shaking. Followed by a low rumbling in the chest. Then, a thin snarl and show of tiny, sharp teeth. And finally, a snapping lunge at whatever hand inched too close. I'm telling you, mean as the dickens.

Most of us have a little Chico inside of us, don't we? When areas of insecurity in our lives feel threatened, we start growling and showing teeth. Sharp teeth. Maybe we're insecure about the way we look. Or our lack of education or success. Could be our family background, economic status, or lack of social polish. Might be an I.Q. deficit. Or a talent deficit. Or a spouse deficit. Could be our standing in the community, or our church, or our family. Or, of course, it could be one of a hundred other unrecognized areas where we feel worthless, less-than, or just not good enough.

And if anyone dares to reach out and touch these sensitive insecurities with thoughtless words or inappropriate actions or sarcastic put-downs, better watch out. The vicious Chico in our hearts might show up, lashing out at any potential threat. Trying to give as good as we get, yanking down their value and pointing out all the not-good-enoughs we know about in their lives. As you can imagine, not very favorable to building a culture of honor.

Insecurities in our lives, no matter how small, can be the greatest hindrance we face when trying to walk out our call to honor all people.

King Saul suffered from Chico syndrome. This big, handsome, popular, prophet-picked warrior and king had a tiny, insecure chihuahua heart. When facing a fierce Philistine giant in the valley of Elah, he shirked his kingly duty, running away in fear. Forty days in a row. When all the women sang more honoring songs about a young shepherd boy who saved the day, he threw his spear in a fit of jealous rage. When his people-pleasing heart was given a choice, he made the wrong one, the sound of bleating sheep eventually giving him away. And when his mantle of authority to rule was removed by God, he chased his successor around the country, focused on keeping what he had instead of ending well with even more.

King David, on the other hand, didn't have a single Chico bone in his body. And this short, red-faced young man had some very solid grounds for feeling insecure. Rejected for some reason by his parents (see Psalm 27:10), he was relegated to watching sheep while wanting to be a warrior, and forgotten in the field when Samuel came calling with his king-anointing oil. Yet David still somehow managed to blossom.

Noticeably stunned by the sight of all the Chico-hearted warriors of Israel running from the giant, King Saul leading the way, David was rebuked and humiliated by his older brothers. For all to see and hear. And he somehow rose above it.

Told by his hero that he was not big enough, strong enough, old enough, experienced enough, or equipped enough to defeat the mighty Philistine warrior, David didn't bow to doubt. And somehow brushed off the slights without a single Chico outburst.

Finally, on the battlefield, in the valley of Elah, he faced the derision and insults and very real death threats from a nine-foot tall Goliath. And somehow, someway, the young shepherd took the giant's head and walked into his God-given destiny. Not an ounce of insecurity in sight.

There was one huge difference between David and King Saul. One huge difference between David and his brothers. One huge difference between David and all the other warriors in Israel on that battlefield. They knew about God, but David knew God. They knew who He was from their ancient manuscripts and stories, but David knew God from his fresh encounters with Him in the field. From the Father's lips straight to the shepherd boy's heart. Which was the secret to his deep, powerful, Chico-resistant security. It's your secret as well.

In Psalm 34:8, David wrote, "Taste and see that the Lord is good." Reading, hearing, and studying about God's ways are so, so important, but they aren't enough to bring about the kind of revelation that produces a deep-rooted, unshakeable security. That comes from taste and see. That comes from relationship. A dwelling in His presence kind of relationship. From His lips to your heart.

When you encounter your Father in relationship instead of just words on a page or sermons on the internet, truth comes alive. About who He really is and what He really thinks about you. And that irritating Chico snarl will slowly fade away, because you won't have any more insecurities in your heart that can be threatened.

And kingdom honor can flow.

CHAPTER TWENTY-THREE
DESTINATION DISEASE

I need to end this book with a bit of a confession. I have a terminal case of destination disease. It's not fatal, just terminal. I hate journeys. For me, they're something to be endured, not enjoyed. Get me where I'm going and I'll be just fine.

When Eva and I are driving on blind, narrow mountain roads in Taiwan on short vacations, she will often look up and say, "Isn't that mountain beautiful?! Let's pull over and take some pictures!" And like a good husband, I'll smile and say "It's gorgeous, Eva." (And might even pull over for the pics.) But inside, all I can think is, "The hotel, the hotel, the hotel! Let's just get to the hotel. That's where the vacation begins."

And when we get in the car to go to the airport to board the huge plane for our twenty plus hour flights to Dallas or Kansas City, all I can think is, "Let's just get there already!" I don't care about all the interesting people we might meet or how many free movies we have access to or how good the airplane food is. I just want to land at my final destination and crawl into a friendly bed. Is that too much to ask?

Problem is, in focusing on the destination, I often miss out on the journey. And the journey is where life happens. Where lessons are learned.

I remember a horrific (to me) flight from Japan to Houston, the big problem being our final destination was supposed to be Dallas, not Houston. Storms in the area changed everything. We landed late in the afternoon, waited in the plane a bit longer than normal, and finally embarked, shuffling off with our bags to immigration. And met a line. A really long line. Eva and I trudged slowly along for five hours to get our passports stamped, and by then, the airport was shutting down. No more flights, and few options for nearby hotels to spend the night. My destination disease was in full-blown overload. "The hotel, the hotel, the hotel! Let's just get to the hotel! Even a Houston hotel!"

The next morning, we went down to the tiny lobby for our free breakfast and met one of the most interesting women we've ever met. At eighty years old, she'd just driven by herself all the way from Austin to Houston. No mean feat. And this lady was a fireball. Totally into diet and fitness, which, of course, endeared her to Eva in a special way. We had such an encouraging breakfast conversation with her. All part of the journey, though not the intended destination.

Which brings us to our high kingdom calling to "honor all people." I have destination disease, so most everything in this book has been about the destination. What does

Jesus-style honor look like? Why is it so important? What do we need to change about our thinking or actions that can help us to walk in this kind of honor? What are the hindrances we should look out for, and what are the keys to success? How can we reach our final destination of honoring all people? But please hear my heart in this: While our destination is important, keeping us on track, headed the right direction, we actually learn true Jesus-style honor through the journey itself.

From some of the stories I've told about myself, you should be able to figure out I'm still in the middle of this important journey. Still learning. Still growing. Still failing at times. But getting up off the ground when I fall and pressing on. As Paul wrote in Philippians 3:13b, "One thing I do: Forgetting what is behind and straining toward what is ahead." (NIV) That's how we learn to walk in this high, high calling Jesus has for us. Get up. Forget the failures. Press on.

Remember in my introduction where I established our calling from I Peter 2:17 to honor all people? "Don't let its size or simplicity fool you, this is one of the most profound commands in the Bible. Might also be one of the most challenging. Might also be one of the most powerful." I still agree with every one of these words.

Now, let's see. If you glance back at Chapter Nineteen, you'll notice that I already have you hanging Matthew 20:28 on your bathroom mirror and Philippians 2:3-7 on your refrigerator door. Time to make some room, maybe on your smartphone, for a special daily honor declaration. Something to remind you of the journey you're on right now to "honor all people." Something to keep the standard of Jesus-style honor as high and alive in your heart as it's supposed to be.

Here it is:

"I will treat everyone I meet today as the precious treasures of God that they are. I will accept them, honor them, encourage them, appreciate them, edify them, and speak life and hope into their hearts. They are priceless masterpieces of their heavenly Father, sons and daughters created in His image for His eternal purposes, and I will love them and value them the same way He does."

**Now, go, go, go! Embrace the journey.
Honor all people. Change the world.**